W9-CDK-373

# How to Develop a Professional Portfolio

Fourth Edition

# How to Develop a Professional Portfolio

## A Manual for Teachers

Dorothy M. Campbell
Pamela Bondi Cignetti
Beverly J. Melenyzer
Diane H. Nettles
Richard M. Wyman, Jr.
*California University of Pennsylvania*

PEARSON

Boston  New York  San Francisco
Mexico City  Montreal  Toronto  London  Madrid  Munich  Paris
Hong Kong  Singapore  Tokyo  Cape Town  Sydney

Executive Editor and Publisher: Stephen D. Dragin
Series Editorial Assistant: Meaghan Minnick
Marketing Manager: Tara Kelly
Production Editor: Gregory Erb
Editorial Production Service: Walsh & Associates, Inc.
Composition Buyer: Linda Cox
Manufacturing Buyer: Megan Cochran
Electronic Composition: Peggy Cabot
Cover Designer: Kristina Mose-Libon

For related titles and support materials, visit our online catalog at www.ablongman.com.

Copyright © 2007, 2004, 2001, 1997 Pearson Education, Inc.

All rights reserved. No part of the material protected by this copyright notice may be reproduced or utilized in any form or by any means, electronic or mechanical, including photocopying, recording, or by any information storage and retrieval system, without written permission from the copyright owner.

To obtain permission(s) to use material from this work, please submit a written request to Allyn and Bacon, Permissions Department, 75 Arlington Street, Boston, MA 02116 or fax your request to 617-848-7320.

Between the time website information is gathered and then published, it is not unusual for some sites to have closed. Also, the transcription of URLs can result in typographical errors. The publisher would appreciate notification where these errors occur so that they may be corrected in subsequent editions.

**Library of Congress Cataloging-in-Publication Data**

How to develop a professional portfolio : a manual for teachers / Dorothy M.
    Campbell . . . [et al.].—4th ed.
        p. cm.
    Includes bibliographic references.
    ISBN 0-205-49100-6
    1. Teachers—Rating of—Handbooks, manuals, etc.   2. Portfolios in education—
Handbooks, manuals, etc.   3. Teachers—Employment—Handbooks, manuals, etc.
I. Campbell, Dorothy M.
LB2838.H56  2006
371.14'4—dc22                                                        2005056381

Printed in the United States of America

10  9  8  7  6  5  4  3  2  1      10  09  08  07  06

# Contents

**Organization of Portfolios around Teaching Standards**     *33*

**Using the Portfolio throughout a Teaching Career**     *61*

**Artifact Possibilities**     *89*

**Appendices**     *103*

# Preface

Why should I create a professional portfolio?

This is a question that has many answers. Here are some of them:

- With your portfolio, you can show your professors what you have learned as you complete a university teacher education program.
- As you collect documents for your portfolio, you can plan your own professional development because you gain insights into your strengths and weaknesses.
- If you are looking for a teaching position, you can showcase your skills and knowledge to prospective employers through your portfolio.
- If you are a new teacher, you can record your new experiences and growing capabilities for administrators through your portfolio.
- If you are a veteran teacher, you can prepare for recertification or professional advancement through a portfolio.
- If you are preparing for National Board Certification, or if you are thinking of doing so, you can record your competencies in teaching standards in a portfolio.

Whether you are a student teacher, a new teacher, a veteran teacher, or a master teacher, this book can help you answer questions you may have about creating your professional portfolio. Since it was first published in 1997, this book has provided thousands of preservice and inservice teachers with specific guidelines needed for organizing a portfolio that documents the achievement of professional goals. Through the use of portfolios that are designed around selected teaching standards, preservice and inservice teachers have provided faculty and credentialing agents with assessments that are goal-based, authentic, and comprehensive. We have reflected on our own experiences with these teachers, as well as with school administrators who have used portfolios effectively in their everyday work.

As a result, we are able to present you some practical tips on pursuing this professional endeavor.

In Chapter 1, you will learn why a portfolio is vital to the optimal professional growth of teachers. Chapter 2 gives you step-by-step procedures for creating a working portfolio and making it evolve into a presentation portfolio. You will learn about electronic portfolio development in Chapter 3, with updated resources that are new to this edition. Chapter 4 is where you will learn about ten standards or principles of teaching, provided by the Interstate New Teacher Assessment and Support Consortium (INTASC) since 1992. Using the INTASC standards as one example, we show you how to build your portfolio around any set of standards, a critical tool in proving your abilities as a teacher. The full potential of the professional portfolio lies in its use throughout your entire teaching career; therefore, we show you how to do this in Chapter 5. In Chapter 6, you will find descriptions of more than fifty possible artifact categories that you can use for documenting your skills, knowledge, and dispositions as a teacher.

This fourth edition offers some new advantages. First, you will find that this book is more interactive than past editions. Each chapter contains a new feature called "Try This," which gives you some step-by-step directions for activities that will help you get started in creating your portfolio. Second, you will find that the examples of rationale pages for portfolio documents are more clearly identified and reader-friendly.

The time to start your portfolio is now. To achieve its full advantages, you will need to view portfolio work as an ongoing process that enables you to chart your growth, set new goals, and design new paths for your professional development. When you treat portfolio work as a culminating event, you will only organize and justify documentation of what you have already done well. Make your portfolio as much an "improving tool" as a "proving tool." Let it reflect you as a growing, changing professional who is committed to continuous improvement.

Teacher education faculty who are developing portfolio assessment systems in their programs usually have many questions that go beyond the scope of this book: questions about performance assessments, rubrics for evaluating portfolios, and comprehensive assessment systems. The challenges facing teacher education programs are addressed in the book *Portfolio and Performance Assessment in Teacher Education* (Campbell, Melenyzer, Nettles, & Wyman, 2000, Allyn and Bacon). This companion piece describes the workings of a portfolio and performance system that holds teacher education majors accountable for achievement of complex teaching tasks. The authors of this book for teacher educators describe four critical elements of a portfolio and performance assessment system: (1) establishing and communicating through program parameters; (2) monitoring the quality of student learning through course-embedded performance assessments and rubrics; (3) supporting students using strategies such as mentoring, work in professional development sites, and portfolio checkpoints; and (4) developing a comprehensive plan for assessment of candidates as well as the teacher education program.

Unlike several years ago when the first edition of this book was published, portfolios are now commonplace in the teacher education field. Preservice and inservice teachers are generally expected to have a professional portfolio that shows their capabilities in teacher behaviors that are reflected in state and national standards. The National Council for Accreditation of Teacher Education (NCATE) evaluates teacher education programs based on the performances of their teacher candidates. A well-developed professional portfolio, organized around standards, is the perfect vehicle for documenting growing competence as a teacher. This book shows you how.

## Acknowledgments

The authors would like to thank the following reviewers of this edition for their input and their time: Laurie M. Hawke, Tarleton State University; Dennis M. Holt, University of North Florida; DeAnn Miller-Boschert, North Dakota State University; and Susan Wyatt, Eastfield College.

# How to Develop a Professional Portfolio

# 1

# What You Need to Know about Portfolios

## Why Portfolios?

Katie Smith sat at the end of a large conference table, surrounded by interviewers, all of whom were administrators or veteran teachers in the school district to which she was applying. Each of them had in front of them a brochure, called "Portfolio at a Glance," which Katie had prepared and mailed to the district personnel office a week ago. This brochure briefly summarized several of the documents in Katie's professional portfolio—her notebook full of documents as well as her electronic portfolio, which contained the same documents in computer files. Its purpose was to capture the highlights of her preservice experiences, as showcased in her portfolio. She used the brochure as a way of introducing herself and her portfolio to her prospective employers. Katie also had with her the notebook that contained the hard-copy contents of her portfolio, as well as a compact disk on which her electronic portfolio was stored.

One of the principals at the table began the interview. He said, "Ms. Smith, I see from your brochure that you have had some experience working in the middle school. Tell us about this."

"Well," said Katie, "I completed the first half of my student teaching assignment in the middle school, in which I taught seventh-grade social studies and language arts classes. I had a wonderful experience, because I was able to use so many of the strategies that I had learned in my methods courses at the university. My supervising teacher encouraged me to use constructivist strategies, along with cooperative learning. I'm so glad that I did, because I found that seventh graders need to be actively involved in their learning, just as the younger children do. As you can see in my brochure, I outlined one of the lessons that I taught in the social studies class. During this lesson, the students researched then reenacted the Boston Tea Party. One of the district goals is for them to retell important events in the Revolutionary War period, so I thought that role playing and drama would enhance their memory of dates and people. I have photographs of this lesson in the portfolio that I brought with me today. Here, I can find them for you."

Katie quickly turned to a page in her portfolio and put a bookmarker on the page. She handed it to the principal.

"A videotape of this lesson is included in my electronic portfolio, which is on this disk," she continued. "You can access the file and view it at your leisure, if you wish."

The principal leaned back in his chair as he examined the document. "Hmm, interesting," he said. "I would like to see your electronic portfolio, too. But first, tell me, how did you manage the behavior of all those seventh graders while they completed this reenactment?"

Katie smiled. "I was a little nervous at first. But I knew that if my students saw a purpose for their learning, and if they were able to make some of their own choices in the project, their interest would be high and I'd have fewer problems with misbehavior. And it worked! In fact, my supervising teacher spoke highly of my classroom management abilities in his evaluation of me. I included a copy of this evaluation in my portfolio, under Standard Five, 'Classroom Management Skills.'"

As Katie spoke, the interviewers passed her portfolio around the table, examining documents and making notes.

After several other questions and more examination of her portfolio, the personnel superintendent said, "Ms. Smith, you were one of several candidates for this position with a well-organized portfolio. Your verbal responses to our questions were excellent but so were those of other candidates. However, your portfolio was unique because it enabled you to support those responses with concrete examples of your knowledge and experience. Your electronic portfolio is also impressive, not only because it shows your abilities with computer technology, but also because it gives us a quick and convenient way to find your documents. Other candidates for this position had portfolios—even electronic ones—but yours was the only one organized around national teaching standards to show your capabilities in the teaching behaviors that we think are important. We are all very impressed. I think you'll make a fine addition to our district teaching faculty."

The preceding scenario makes evident how imperative it is that, as a prospective teacher, you are able to demonstrate your teaching competence to others in concrete ways. Teaching jobs are highly competitive, and therefore creative ways of presenting yourself are essential.

However, prospective employers are not the only ones who will be holding you accountable for proving your competence. State departments of education are increasing requirements for compelling evidence of performance before issuing teacher certification. In addition, in 1987, a National Board for Professional

Teaching Standards was formed for the purpose of setting standards for the teaching profession, thus impacting teacher certification. A voluntary national teaching credential is now a real possibility. Many teacher education programs are utilizing measurements of performance as an alternative for evaluating preservice teachers' progress in their professional training. Furthermore, once you obtain a teaching job, you will be periodically evaluated and held accountable for utilizing exemplary teaching practices throughout your professional career.

Traditionally, assessments such as test scores and transcript grades have been used to evaluate teachers. However, you will find that these types of assessments do not necessarily reflect the range of abilities that true professionals possess. Teachers are justifiably concerned that assessments and accountability requirements be authentic, broad-based, and impartial. As a professional, you will want all of your knowledge and experience to be taken into account when you are evaluated.

One characteristic of excellent teachers is that they learn from every experience and every person they meet. They seek ongoing professional training to refine their practice. They remain current about educational research. They read professional journals and books, attend workshops, and interact with colleagues in order to benefit from the experience of others. They ask endless questions of other people and really listen to the answers. They try out new ideas, reflect on the results, and then discard or adapt the ideas. Often they keep reflective journals. When they travel, they look for opportunities to learn all they can about other places. They volunteer in the community, getting to know its people, values, and agencies. When they join groups, they tend to be the ones who go to the meetings and do the committee work.

Although teachers know that all these forms of experience have contributed to their becoming effective professionals, most would find it difficult to demonstrate to others exactly how these various experiences have fit into their pattern of professional growth. As you embark on your professional journey, you will probably find that you, too, have many valuable skills and experiences that are difficult to convey in a single test score or course grade. Because these skills and experiences are part of your growing competencies, it is important that you be able to convey them to others.

A professional portfolio can help. It can be a tool that enables you to make sense out of a myriad of experiences. It also can bring into focus a clear picture of yourself as a growing, changing professional. Equally as significant, it can be a convincing, effective vehicle for you to demonstrate to others in a meaningful way the skills and knowledge you have gained in something as complex as teaching.

## What Is a Portfolio?

A portfolio is an organized, goal-driven documentation of your professional growth and achieved competence in the complex act called teaching. It is a collection of documents that provides tangible evidence of the wide range of knowledge, dispositions, and skills that you possess as a growing professional. What's more, documents in the portfolio are self-selected, reflecting your individuality and autonomy. Therefore, a portfolio is not merely a file of course projects and assignments, nor is it a scrapbook of teaching memorabilia.

There are actually two kinds of portfolios that you will be developing: a working portfolio and a presentation portfolio. A working portfolio is characterized by your ongoing systematic collection of selected work in courses and evidence of community activities. This collection would form a framework for self-assessment and goal setting. Later, you would develop a presentation portfolio by winnowing your collection to samples of your work that best reflect your achieved competence, individuality, and creativity as a professional educator.

## What Is a Working Portfolio?

A working portfolio contains unabridged versions of the documents you have carefully selected to portray your professional growth. It is always much larger and more complete than a presentation portfolio. For example, it might contain entire reflective journals, complete units, unique teacher-made materials, and a collection of videos of your teaching. Working portfolios are often stored in a combination of computer disks, notebooks, and even boxes.

## What Is a Presentation Portfolio?

A presentation portfolio is compiled for the expressed purpose of giving others an effective and easy-to-read portrait of your professional competence. A presentation portfolio is selective and streamlined because other people usually do not have the time to review all the material in your working portfolio. This holds true whether it is a paper-based portfolio or an electronic one.

If you have chosen to create a paper-based portfolio, we recommend the use of a notebook, in which you insert only the most pertinent documents needed to showcase your abilities. If you have decided to create an electronic portfolio, you will find that it is easier to include a greater number and variety of documents; however, you will need to be sure to catalogue them distinctly and accurately on your homepage, disk, or CD.

In making a presentation portfolio, you will find that less is more. For example, since you would be unlikely to take to an interview all your teacher-made learning materials, you might rely on either paper or digital photographs. If you have a video of your classroom teaching, make sure it is well-edited and annotated, then insert it into a pocket of your paper-based portfolio or add it to your electronic portfolio. If you have a large project that you wish to include in your portfolio, you can simply edit it for an electronic portfolio, but it may be necessary to streamline it to sample pages only for a paper-based portfolio.

The working portfolio and the presentation portfolio differ in that all documents in a presentation portfolio should be preceded by an explanation of the importance or relevance of the document so that the reviewer understands the context of your work.

## How Do I Organize My Portfolio?

There is one essential way in which working portfolios and presentation portfolios are alike. From their inception, both need to have a well-established organizational system. There is no one standard way to organize a portfolio, but to be effective it must have a system of organization that is understandable and meaningful to you and other educators. We suggest organizing your portfolio around a set of goals you are trying to achieve. This makes sense when one of your purposes for a portfolio is to demonstrate to others that you are achieving success in meeting standards set for excellence in the teaching profession.

Many professional organizations are setting goals for the teachers of the twenty-first century. These organizations include state departments of education, professional societies such as the National Association for the Education of Young Children or the National Council of Teachers of Mathematics, interagency groups, and university schools of education. Appendix A provides website addresses for many professional organizations concerned with standards for teaching. The professional goals established by these organizations are called by a variety of names, including standards, principles, performance domains, outcomes, and competencies. They are all attempts to reflect the knowledge, skills, and dispositions that define excellent teachers and therefore are goals for you to achieve.

You should become familiar with a number of documents that outline sets of standards for your discipline, your state, and your own university department. As you study these standards, choose or adapt a set of goals that makes sense to you in your particular situation. Regardless of the goals or standards chosen, everything collected for your portfolio should be organized around the chosen goal statements.

The sample goals or standards used in this book are principles established by the Interstate New Teacher Assessment and Support Consortium (INTASC).[1] These standards were chosen because of their general applicability for teachers of all disciplines and all levels, preschool to grade twelve. It is apparent that engaging in the development of a portfolio organized around a set of goals or standards will

---

[1]Darling-Hammond, L. (Ed.) (1992, September). *Model standards for beginning teacher licensing and development: A resource for state dialogue.* Unpublished draft, Interstate New Teacher Assessment and Support Consortium, Council of Chief State School Officers, Washington, DC.

greatly facilitate your growth and achievement in the goals identified. Figure 1.1 shows the INTASC standards.

## What Evidence Should I Include in My Portfolio?

For every standard, you will include artifacts that demonstrate you have met this principle. An artifact is tangible evidence of knowledge that is gained, skills that are mastered, values that are clarified, or dispositions and attitudes that are characteristic of you. Artifacts cannot conclusively prove the attainment of knowledge, skills, or dispositions, but they provide indicators of achieved competence. For example, lesson and unit plans are pieces of evidence that might provide strong indication of your ability to plan curriculum or use a variety of teaching strategies. A video of your teaching might be a convincing indicator of your ability to manage and motivate a group of students. The same artifact may document more than one standard. Chapter 6 will describe more than fifty possibilities for portfolio artifacts. At first, you will collect many artifacts. Later, you will need to place artifacts selectively within each of the standards. Those artifacts that represent your growth and very best professional work should be included as evidence in your professional portfolio. Ask yourself: Would I be proud to have my future employer and peer group see this? Is this an example of what my future professional work might look like? Does this represent what I stand for as a professional educator? If not, what can I do to revise or rearrange so that it represents my best efforts?

## Who Is the Audience for My Portfolio?

Information contained in the portfolio will be of interest to individuals who will be assessing your performance and measuring your accountability. While a student, your portfolio will be reviewed by your university faculty and advisors. Moreover, your portfolio will be an excellent way for you to introduce yourself to cooperating teachers and administrators during field experiences and student teaching. During job interviews, your portfolio is likely to be reviewed by superintendents, principals, teachers, and in some cases even school board members. As you begin your teaching career, your portfolio will be a helpful vehicle for mentors, in-service education coordinators, and other colleagues. In some school districts, a portfolio will be relied on by supervisory staff charting ongoing career development or making tenure and promotion decisions. There is also a good possibility that your portfolio will one day be used to facilitate licensing by professional organizations, state agencies, or national consortiums. Most importantly, the portfolio provides you, the author, with an informative and accurate picture of your professional development and growth.

The standards below were developed by Interstate New Teacher Assessment and Support Consortium (INTASC). The designated headings are ours.

✓*Standard One—Knowledge of Subject Matter* **need 1**
The teacher understands the central concepts, tools of inquiry, and structures of the discipline(s) he or she teaches and can create learning experiences that make these aspects of subject matter meaningful for students.

✓*Standard Two—Knowledge of Human Development and Learning* **2**
The teacher understands how children learn and develop and can provide learning opportunities that support their intellectual, social, and personal development.

✓*Standard Three—Adapting Instruction for Individual Needs*
The teacher understands how students differ in their approaches to learning and creates instructional opportunities that are adapted to diverse learners.

*Standard Four—Multiple Instructional Strategies* **need**
The teacher understands and uses a variety of instructional strategies to encourage students' development of critical thinking, problem solving, and performance skills.

✓*Standard Five—Classroom Motivation and Management Skills* **2**
The teacher uses an understanding of individual and group motivation and behavior to create a learning environment that encourages positive social interaction, active engagement in learning, and self-motivation.

*Standard Six—Communication Skills* **replace 2**
The teacher uses knowledge of effective verbal, nonverbal, and media communication techniques to foster active inquiry, collaboration, and supportive interaction in the classroom.

*Standard Seven—Instructional Planning Skills* **need**
The teacher plans instruction based on knowledge of subject matter, students, the community, and curriculum goals.

*Standard Eight—Assessment of Student Learning* **1**
The teacher understands and uses formal and informal assessment strategies to ensure the continuous intellectual, social, and physical development of the learner.

*Standard Nine—Professional Commitment and Responsibility* **1**
The teacher is a reflective practitioner who continually evaluates the effects of his or her choices and actions on others (students, parents, and other professionals in the learning community) and who actively seeks out opportunities to grow professionally.

*Standard Ten—Partnerships* **2**
The teacher fosters relationships with school colleagues, parents, and agencies in the larger community to support students' learning and well-being.

**FIGURE 1.1**  Model Standards for Beginning Teachers' Licensing and Development

# How Might I Use My Portfolio?

In this chapter you have been introduced to a very motivating reason for you to commit time, energy, and thought to developing a portfolio: You will have a high-impact, authentic product by which your professional competence can be judged by others. Before you get into later chapters, which will provide you with detailed steps and examples for developing a portfolio, you might reflect on other ways beyond interviews and certification requirements to use your portfolio to your best advantage.

You will find as you engage in portfolio development that you will gain a much clearer picture of yourself as an emerging professional. Your portfolio will provide a record of quantitative and qualitative growth over time in your selected goal areas or standards. You will have in hand a trail of evidence of your progress in each of your teaching standards. This will give you a gratifying sense of accomplishment and pride and will help you have ever-increasing confidence in your professional abilities.

As you review this record of your professional growth, you will also gain a vision of the big picture. You will more fully understand who you want to be as a professional (as defined by the standards that you choose). Then, as you organize selected artifacts around these standards, you will begin to discern a pattern of how your various course assignments and out-of-class experiences fit into this big picture and contributed to your development.

As you gain more self-understanding, your portfolio will empower you to assume more control over your own future learning. You will be well equipped to collaborate with professors in individualizing assignments or with advisors in planning courses of study. You will have a greatly expanded resume to be used to introduce yourself to cooperating teachers and administrators in student teaching and field experiences classes. You and your cooperating teachers now have a tool for determining the most appropriate teaching experiences for you. As you can see, when you reflect on the portrait your portfolio provides, you will be well positioned to set realistic and meaningful goals for yourself. Choices that exist in your coursework, field work, and self-initiated learning opportunities will now have a meaningful focus.

In addition, the portfolio may be used by a university program as a way to keep students and faculty focused on goals or standards valued by the program. Students will be continually reflecting on the standards as their portfolios provide an authentic and meaningful way to be assessed professionally. Portfolios will provide faculty members with evidence of their effectiveness in preparing students to meet selected standards. Portfolios can help with program evaluation and bring to light the need for new courses, revised course syllabi, or policy changes.

It should now be clear why having a professional portfolio is of value, what a portfolio is, what goes into one, and who would be interested in seeing it. Now you are ready to look at portfolio development in a more specific way.

## TRY THIS

**Writing an Autobiographical Sketch**

A good way to start your portfolio is with a one-page autobiographical sketch or self-introduction. This might be in the form of a written narrative or a letter. This piece should provide the readers of your portfolio with some information about you that is not readily apparent from a resume or even from your collection of artifacts. There are several possibilities to consider as you write this. Think about the categories and questions shown below, because they may help you compose your autobiographical sketch.

*Why You Chose to Become a Teacher*
- Have you had a lifelong dream of becoming a teacher?
- What set of circumstances in your life brought you into the teaching field?
- Who influenced you most as you were growing up or as you were making decisions about your life's work?

*Your Personal Attributes*
- What attributes do you have that would make you a good teacher?
- Are you a warm and nurturing person who is especially encouraging to others?
- Do you have a professional demeanor and business-like attitude?
- Do you hold high expectations for your own success and for the success of your students?
- Have you overcome some personal obstacles that would help you empathize with students who must do the same thing?
- Have you had unique experiences or travels that would enhance your students' experiences in your classroom?

*Your Long-Term Goals and Ambitions*
- Where do you see yourself in five years? Ten years?
- What ambitions do you have as an educator?
- How will your goals and ambitions make you a better teacher?

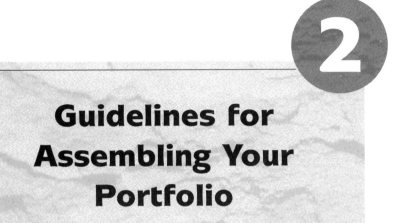

# Guidelines for Assembling Your Portfolio

## How to Use This Chapter

Creating a portfolio is not difficult—it just takes time and personal reflection. As stated in Chapter 1, the process of developing a portfolio begins early in your professional career, when you start to collect documents and pieces of your work that exemplify your capabilities as a teacher. This collection, called the working portfolio, will be extensive; it will contain everything you have done that you judge to be worthy of saving. Eventually, you will need to produce a presentation portfolio. This is for the purpose of showcasing only portions of your work for a prospective employer or certification officer. The presentation portfolio is streamlined; only the most pertinent material for the position is organized and displayed. Both types of portfolios are organized in the same manner: Documents are categorized by standards that you have adopted. These standards are goals that will guide you throughout your teacher preparation work, your career, or both. This chapter will give you some practical information on putting together both types of portfolios.

The first section of the chapter contains information to help you organize your collection of documents for a working portfolio. This will be an ongoing project as you complete your teacher education program or prepare for certification. The second section is designed to help you produce a presentation portfolio that is uniquely yours, at the same time documenting important information that will be examined by prospective employers or certification officers. Included are questions you may have about assembling your portfolio. The answers provide guidelines that are important; however, feel free to use your own creativity in developing a portfolio that portrays you as an individual as well as a professional educator.

# Creating the Working Portfolio

## Where Do I Start?

Choose a way to store your documents. The working portfolio will contain a multitude of artifacts, many of which will be cumbersome. Decide how you want to house your artifacts. This portfolio needs to be easily accessible, expandable, and organized. You may want to use a large file box. Office supply stores carry cardboard banker's boxes, which are easily assembled and easy to carry around. You can put all your artifacts in one box, with files dividing it into sections. If you prefer, you can use several smaller boxes, one for each standard you are documenting. Other options are to use a large notebook that can be divided into sections or a file drawer in a cabinet that has plenty of space for several folders. Rather than always storing hard copies, you might opt to save many documents in digital format.

Consider the types of artifacts you will be saving when making this decision. Will you be using a number of videotapes? Will you be making teaching materials you will want to save? Will you be taking photographs of projects? Do you tend to write lengthy papers? These types of artifacts require space as well as special types of handling when organizing and storing them for long periods of time.

## How Do I Document the Standards?

**Create a Filing System.**   Your portfolio will contain several sections, each of which will correspond to a standard you have adopted. In the examples provided in this book, each section will reflect one of the ten standards outlined by the Interstate New Teacher Assessment and Support Consortium (INTASC). These standards are descriptions of teacher behaviors agreed upon by a group of educators in the consortium. They were developed to be compatible with other national standards for certification. If you are a teacher education student, your school program has probably adopted a set of goals or standards that guides its students. Such a set of goals is useful for guiding preservice teachers through their teacher preparation program at the university or for guiding inservice teachers as they apply for recertification. Adopt a set of standards appropriate for your situation and organize the portfolios around these standards.

Your portfolio needs to document that you have indeed met your chosen goals. Therefore, organize your portfolio in such a way that these standards are easily identified. If you are using a file box or expanding file for your working portfolio, create a file or section for each standard. You may want to color code the files to facilitate easier management. If you are using a notebook to house your working portfolio, the best way to do this is to include tab pages for each standard, dividing your portfolio into as many sections as there are standards. You may wish to maintain an electronic file for each standard.

**Examine the Possibilities for Documentation.**   Study the suggestions and examples in this manual. Sample standard statements are listed and explained in Chapter 4 along with real-life examples. In Chapter 6, many possible artifacts are listed. These are artifacts that could be used to document any set of standards. They have been defined and explained, so that you can get some idea of what is meant by terms such as "video scenario critiques" or "theme studies" and also so that you can see the possibilities for documenting standards. Check your files for any of these artifacts and save them. Many of them probably reflect class assignments given in your methods classes. However, you may want to create artifacts. For example, perhaps you have not already written a philosophy statement, even though you have a very clear idea of your philosophy of education. Therefore, composing one for the purpose of including it in the portfolio would be a wise idea. You may also need to add to artifacts you already have. Suppose you attended a professional meeting or lecture but did not write a reaction paper or take notes. Now is a good time to write a brief critique of what you saw and heard and add it to your file for the portfolio.

**Become a Pack Rat.**   If you have not already done so, begin collecting. Organize your file box, cabinet, disks, or notebook and start putting examples of class assignments and other artifacts in appropriate categories right away. This is necessary because you will want to see if there are any standards for which you do not have artifacts, something that is discussed in the next section. Remember that you can use an artifact in more than one section because several types of artifacts may document more than one standard. If this happens, photocopy the artifact and highlight the part that specifically addresses the standard. One note of caution: Use this photocopying and highlighting idea sparingly. Duplicating too many artifacts will make your portfolio look as if you do not use a variety of experiences.

As you file each of your artifacts under a standard, make brief notes about why you have filed the document under that particular standard. These notes can be used later when you are ready to create your presentation portfolio. At that time, you will need to write a rationale for each artifact. This is a brief statement that explains why the artifact you chose for the standard is appropriate and how the artifact showcases your competence in that area. From the standard statement, use specific descriptors that will jar your memory and connect the artifact to the standard. You may want to write these notes on an index card and clip the card to the document. Figure 2.1 shows an example of notes written for a case study that could be used to document INTASC Standard Two.

**Look for Holes.**   Standards that are not well documented by your artifacts will become evident as you collect and categorize materials. Keep the standards in mind as you take other courses or participate in professional activities. Whenever

---

*Standard Two—Case Study*
- Shows how a child's language developed from infancy
- Written over a 3-month period
- Identifies some stages of language development
- Shows how the child learned several new words

---

**FIGURE 2.1** Example of a Note Card to Attach to the Artifact When Filing in the Working Portfolio

you have assignment choices, such as journal article critiques to write or projects to complete in your university coursework, think about the standards you need to work on. Consider how you can make this assignment document your "missing standard." Look for meetings to attend, journals to read or subscribe to, organizations to join, extra credit assignments to complete, community activities to volunteer for, personal diaries to write, or any number of activities that can be recorded and included in your portfolio. You may also want to ask your professors for guidance in this area. See if they have suggestions for ways to make your class assignments document a particular standard while at the same time completing the requirements for their courses.

One of the ways you can manage the documentation of standards is with the Artifact Checklist in Appendix B. This is a list of all the artifacts defined in Chapter 6. As you use them in your portfolio, mark them with a date on the checklist. Be sure to use a pencil, because as time passes, you may choose to remove some artifacts from your portfolio; thus, you will need to erase the date mark. This checklist allows you (and your professor or advisor) to see at a glance the standards you need to work on. It also allows you to quickly assess your use of artifacts. Are you depending on some types of artifacts more than others? You may want to diversify your artifacts to more clearly document your repertoire of abilities.

## Creating the Presentation Portfolio

### Why Create Another Portfolio?

At various stages in your professional career when you want to showcase your abilities to someone else, you will need a presentation portfolio. You should determine the collection of documents by the audience reviewing the presentation portfolio. For example, in a preservice teacher education program the audience might be faculty and cooperating teachers. Later, you will tailor a presentation portfolio specifically to a job or a type of teaching certification that you are seeking. As an experienced teacher, your presentation portfolio might be used for national board certification, mentoring, managing your own professional growth, or advancing within the profession. Chapter 5 elaborates on these uses of presentation portfolios.

## How Do I Prepare the Presentation Portfolio?

**Use a Container That Works for You.**    For your presentation portfolio, you can experiment with many types of containers such as notebooks, expanding files, folders, computer disks, or portfolio satchels. Consider the types of artifacts you have collected. If you have electronic documents such as videotapes or computer disks, you will need to format them so they are easily accessible and logically organized. When using a hard-copy portfolio, you want your reader to be able to open it and read it without struggling with pages, binders, or pockets. Therefore, use a container that is large enough to house all your documents. Most people choose a large notebook. Generally, 2" or 3" three-ring binders are fine. A professional look is important. Browse through an office supply store for your notebook. Many stores carry a style with a plastic insert cover that you can personalize. Pockets for storage of electronic documents are also available and can be inserted easily in most types of notebooks. One note of caution: Do not use a notebook that is too big, or your portfolio will look empty.

**Identify the Standards.**    Remember that your prospective employer or certification officer might not know what each of the standard titles means. As with the working portfolio, you will need to label each section with an abbreviated title for the standard as well as a copy of the entire standard statement.

**Be Selective in Choosing Artifacts.**    As in the working portfolio, you will gather artifacts that document your abilities in each of the standards you have adopted. However, most reviewers do not have a great deal of time to peruse portfolios and are interested in only the most pertinent information about your abilities. This means you must be selective in what you choose for the presentation portfolio. Two or three artifacts in each section are all you need. Choose artifacts that exemplify the type of position or certificate you are seeking. For example, if you are interviewing for a first-grade teaching position, select as many examples of your work in the area of early childhood education as possible.

**Write a Rationale.**    In each section of your portfolio, you will insert various artifacts that document your proficiency and experience for that standard. However, readers of your portfolio will not necessarily know why you included these particular artifacts. Therefore, you need to include a rationale for each artifact in the notebook. Type a brief statement explaining your justification for including this artifact in the portfolio for this particular standard. This statement should be no longer than one page. Make sure you explain why this is an example of your best work, specifically for this standard. Your rationale should show the reader that you know what you are capable of doing in terms of meeting the standard. Be specific about showcasing your abilities. (This is difficult for some people. They feel as if they are bragging.) Do not simply summarize the document. When writing a rationale, answer these questions:

1. **What?** What is the experience reflected in this document?
2. **What?** What is the artifact?
3. **So what?** What does this work say about my growing competence?
4. **Where and why?** Under which standard is it filed? Why there?
5. **Now what?** What will I do differently in the future? How will the skills I've gained transfer to new experiences?

To organize your portfolio and make artifacts and rationales clearly identifiable, add a rationale page for each artifact you include. This page lists the name of the artifact and the date it was written. If applicable, list the course number for the class in which you completed the assignment. Then, type the rationale statement for the artifact. Figures 2.2 and 2.3 show examples of rationale pages.

**Present Your Artifacts Professionally.**   Remember that this portfolio will represent you as a professional, often in your absence. You will want to make sure your first impression is a good one. Therefore, carefully consider all that goes in this notebook or file. Listed below are questions to ask yourself as you check your work.

*SAMPLE RATIONALE PAGE*

*Artifact for Standard Five: Classroom Motivation and Management*

*Name of Artifact:* Journal Article Critique
*Date:* May 2, XXXX
*Course:* EDE 201—Foundations of Education
*Rationale:*
    I have included this journal article critique on cultural diversity under Standard Five. I feel the critique belongs under this standard because the most important thing I learned from the article was how to build a positive classroom climate through celebrating diversity. For this assignment, I not only summarized the article, but I stated my position on the subject and described how I would address cultural diversity in my classroom. I came to understand that the sharing of different cultures, other than just on holidays and special occasions, helps break down barriers between people. In my future teaching, I will strive to enrich the lives of all my students and enhance the classroom climate through having students share their cultural traditions and viewpoints.

**FIGURE 2.2**   Example of a Rationale Page for a University Course Assignment

## SAMPLE RATIONALE PAGE

*Artifact for Standard Nine: Professional Commitment
and Responsibility*

*Name of Artifact:* Who's Who Among American Teachers Selection Letter
*Date:* March, XXXX
*Rationale:*

    I was recently selected into *Who's Who Among American Teachers.* I received this letter of selection at a time in my career when I could use some encouragement. The nomination letter was written by one of my students. I placed this document under Standard Nine because it helped me to step back and take a look at what I was doing and what I needed to be doing.

    I had what seemed to me one class of rather lazy and apathetic students. I was having a difficult time getting them to do their work or even come to class. I was beginning to get a serious case of "Why do I do this?" when this letter appeared in my mailbox. I read the letter several times and then thought about what I had done to make such an impression on this particular student. I thought about the class that she was in and how active and involved the students in it always were. Her recognition of my teaching efforts meant so much to me and gave me a new goal—to do everything I could to make the class I was struggling with now feel as she did. I began looking at our units with renewed enthusiasm and the desire to live up to the high praise that I had received. I began preparing new activities designed to make these students want to be in class and do the work. By the end of the semester, their grades had greatly improved, along with their attitudes (and mine).

    This one letter helped me realize that I need to constantly work to live up to this award. When I start getting tired or frustrated, I can look back on the impact I had on this one student and feel re-energized and ready to do what it takes to impact someone else in the same way. It was as if I had lost my purpose for teaching somewhere in the content, and Natasha found it, dusted it off, and handed it back to me, as good as new.

**FIGURE 2.3**    Example of a Rationale Page Written by a High School Teacher

1. Have I been careful to present only my own work? (For example, you should not include handouts prepared by someone else for training you've attended.) Have I shared credit for work I've done collaboratively with others?
2. Are spelling and grammar in Standard English?
3. Is all work typed? All rationale pages, tabs, and documents that you create for the portfolio should be typed. Make sure your printer produces clear, dark print. Remember that reviewers will notice your proficiency with word processing. The only exceptions to typed work would be artifacts such as journals, students' papers, or observation logs that were not originally typed.

4. Is everything about your overall presentation consistent? Are lines on your rationale pages either single-spaced or double-spaced consistently throughout?
5. Is your work neat? Avoid use of whiteout or erasures.
6. Is your organization easy to follow? Do you have a table of contents that clearly identifies all parts of the portfolio?

## How Do I Make the Presentation Portfolio Unique?

Your presentation portfolio will be unique because it reflects your abilities, your strengths, your professionalism. No one else will have a portfolio like yours because you have written all the documents in the notebook. Others will be able to see very quickly what you know about teaching and what you believe about education. Listed below are ways to make the portfolio more personalized.

**Be Creative.**    You may wish to add touches of creativity such as pertinent artwork, photographs, or famous quotations. Other embellishments include border paper, clip art, graphic organizers, and captions for photographs. Your rationale pages for each of the artifacts would be good places for these. You can also be creative with the cover of your portfolio, making sure to include all necessary identifying information. Another way to add creativity is to develop the portfolio around a theme. (One we have seen is a portfolio that depicted its writer as a traveler on a journey down the road of professional life.) Whatever you do, keep embellishment simple. Although visual impact is important, overuse of photographs or decorated pages may detract from the professionalism of your documents. You do not want to detract from the work you are trying to showcase, nor do you want to appear as if you are trying to hide incompetence.

**Create a Place for Personal Data.**    As you move through various stages of your professional career, documents in your professional portfolio will change. Some documents, however, are beneficial at any stage. At the beginning of your portfolio, in a well-marked section, include important documents that serve as an introduction. Possibilities are:

1. Letter of introduction or preface to the portfolio
2. Your photograph
3. Biographical sketch
4. Resume
5. Letters of recommendation
6. Transcripts
7. Student teaching evaluations
8. Certification documents
9. Philosophy of education statement

**Create a Table of Contents.** Once you have all the pieces to your presentation portfolio assembled, prepare a table of contents to aid your reviewers. The following is a sample table of contents for a portfolio built around INTASC standards.

**Contents**
*Preface*
*About the Author*
*Philosophy of Education*
*Personal Data*
    Resume
    Letters of Recommendation
    Transcripts
    Student Teaching Evaluations
*Artifacts for Standard One—Knowledge of Subject Matter*
    Science Unit on Geology
    Research Paper on Medieval Times
*Artifacts for Standard Two—Knowledge of Human Development and Learning*
    Case Study of a Seventh-Grade Boy
    Observation Report on Characteristics of Third Graders
*Artifacts for Standard Three—Adapting Instruction for Individual Needs*
    Self-Evaluation of Teaching a Talented and Gifted Group
    Letter of Recommendation on Coaching Multilevel Swimmers
*Artifacts for Standard Four—Multiple Instructional Strategies*
    Cooperative Learning Activity
    Discovery Lesson on Immigration
*Artifacts for Standard Five—Classroom Motivation and Management Skills*
    Behavior Analysis after Implementing a Reward System
    Summary of Workshops on Proactive Classroom Management
*Artifacts for Standard Six—Communication Skills*
    PowerPoint Presentation on Mammals
    Public Speaking Competition Award
*Artifacts for Standard Seven—Instructional Planning Skills*
    Lesson Plan on Money
    Thematic Unit Plan on Natural Disasters
*Artifacts for Standard Eight—Assessment of Student Learning*
    Performance Assessment for Unit on Pond Life
    Chapter Test in Social Studies
*Artifacts for Standard Nine—Professional Commitment and Responsibility*
    Outstanding Student Teacher of the Year Certificate
    Pictures of Afterschool Fitness Program
*Artifacts for Standard Ten—Partnerships*
    Homework Assignments Encouraging Parent Involvement
    Participation Log for Parent Teacher Association
*A Final Word: Reflections on the Past; Goals for the Future*

Remember, the portfolio portrays you as an individual and as a professional. It shows evidence of your own personal insights into your experiences and that you have reflected on what you can do. In short, it is your showcase; use it to your advantage. The next chapter explains how an electronic portfolio can enhance that advantage.

## TRY THIS

### Writing Your First Rationale

Writing a rationale for the first time can be somewhat intimidating. That need not be the case. In fact, rationales have a predictable pattern that makes their composition easier. Once you understand the pattern and the basic questions that rationales answer, you will write them with greater ease. Try writing a rough draft of your first rationale by following these steps in the order presented. This exercise will help you become acquainted with the construction of rationales.

1. Select an experience or a class assignment that you want to showcase in your portfolio because you value the learning that it provided to you.

2. Now you will use the questions on page 16 to help you write your first rationale. Take a look at the first question: **"What is the experience?"** Describe the assignment or experience clearly enough to be understood by a reader of your portfolio who is unfamiliar with your work and your class assignments.

3. Think about your response to the second "what" question: **"What is the artifact?"** Will you use a letter of recommendation, a lesson plan, a summary, or perhaps a research paper to document this experience? Remember that an experience can be documented with more than one artifact. Make a note of the artifact or collection of artifacts that you intend to use.

4. Now make a list that answers the third question: **"So what?"** Write down all the skills, competencies, or understandings that you gained through this experience. How did this experience or class assignment benefit you and better prepare you for teaching? For some experiences you will have one major gain or outcome; for other more complex experiences such as field experiences in classrooms, you will have many competencies that you gained.

5. The next question is: **"Where and why?"** Under what standard will you file this artifact and why there? To answer this question you need to review your list of outcomes in step 4 to see their relation to the standards you are

using. Put a circle around the most important thing you learned from this experience. You should file your work under the standard that best connects to the most important benefit of this experience, even if the experience provided a host of other benefits.

6. Finally, think about this: **"Now what?"** Make notes of ways that you can use what you learned from this experience in your future teaching experiences.

7. Using the notes from steps 2–6, write one or two paragraphs summarizing this information. The order in which you address these guiding questions can vary in your rationales. The important thing is that your paragraphs answer all the questions listed above.

8. You are now ready to create the heading for the rationale. The important thing to remember when naming the artifact in the heading is to use a simple, straightforward title that most clearly communicates the nature of the document. It is also important to remember when supplying the date, that you use the date the experience occurred, not the date the rationale was written.

For additional help with writing rationales, review the two sample rationales in this chapter and the ten sample rationales in Chapter 4.

# Electronic Portfolios

Technology now exists that makes it possible for prospective and practicing teachers to demonstrate teaching competence and professional growth through the use of electronic portfolios. Like a paper-based portfolio, an electronic portfolio is organized around standards and contains artifacts that reflect your growth and best professional work. However, the artifact possibilities for an electronic portfolio are far more diverse. Traditional documents such as lesson and unit plans, research papers, and letters of recommendation can be complemented by video clips of you teaching a lesson or tutoring an individual student, an audio clip of you making a presentation to parents, or a PowerPoint presentation showing your students participating in a social studies simulation. The addition of multimedia artifacts provides the portfolio reviewer with a far richer and more complete picture of you as a growing or accomplished professional.

Electronic portfolios are not for everyone. Creating any kind of portfolio demands a great deal of time and effort. Constructing an electronic portfolio, however, requires specialized skills and equipment you may not possess or have access to. The decision to proceed in developing an electronic portfolio should be undertaken after reflecting upon answers to the following questions:

1. How interested am I in an electronic portfolio?
2. Do I have the necessary technological skills (or know someone who does) to create an electronic portfolio?
3. Do I have access to the necessary equipment and software?
4. Am I willing to invest the substantial amount of energy and time required to develop a well-designed electronic portfolio?

If you are unsure about whether you want to undertake the development of an electronic portfolio, the information in this chapter will assist you in making that decision. If you answered these four questions in the affirmative, what follows will help get you started in the right direction. Since entire texts have been written on the subject, you will probably have to read additional material regarding the technological aspects of electronic portfolio development.

## Definition of Electronic Portfolios

We define a portfolio in Chapter 1 as an organized, goal-driven documentation of your professional growth and teaching competence. It is tangible evidence of the wide range of knowledge, dispositions, and skills that you possess as a professional. An electronic portfolio serves exactly the same purpose, but artifacts are created and presented using electronic technologies and appear in a variety of media formats: audio, video, digital photographs, graphics, and text. Links are created to show the relationship between the artifacts and standards.

An electronic portfolio should serve as your presentation portfolio, the purpose of which is to give others an effective and easy-to-read portrait of your professional competence. In Chapter 5, we describe a number of ways a professional portfolio can be of assistance to you as you proceed through a teacher education program, apply for a teaching position, or seek certification through the National Board of Professional Teaching Standards (NBPTS). These benefits hold true whether your portfolio is paper-based or electronic. An electronic portfolio, however, possesses unique advantages due to its structure and format.

## Benefits of Electronic Portfolios

### Demonstrate Technology Knowledge and Skills

A paper-based portfolio documents your teaching competence and professional growth. An electronic portfolio permits you to showcase both your best work as a professional educator and, additionally, your knowledge and skill with technology. With an electronic portfolio, it is no longer necessary to include artifacts related to the use of technology because the portfolio itself becomes documentation of your facility with computer systems and software.

Virtually every state has adopted standards describing what students should know and be able to do related to technology. As a teacher, you are responsible for ensuring your students meet these standards. An electronic portfolio demonstrates that you possess technological knowledge and skills, thus making it more likely you will incorporate technology into your teaching.

### Facilitate Distribution

As a candidate for a teaching position, you would be understandably reluctant to leave your paper-based portfolio with an interviewer because it contains original documents that are irreplaceable. An electronic portfolio contained on a compact disk (CD-ROM) is easily transportable and readily duplicated, allowing copies to be handed to reviewers at any time and in any situation.

An electronic portfolio on a CD-ROM can be mailed to a principal or super-intendent prior to an interview or, if your portfolio is web-based, you can simply include the URL (web address) in your application cover letter. This allows re-viewers to examine your portfolio prior to the scheduled interview. If given the opportunity to examine the portfolio in advance, interviewers will more likely tailor questions to the contents of your portfolio. This should work to your advantage since it focuses the interview on your documented strengths and competencies.

**Store Many Documents.** As we recommend in Chapter 1, a presentation port-folio should be selective and streamlined because most reviewers do not have either the time or the interest to examine every document in your working port-folio. The structure of an electronic portfolio, however, allows you to include far more than the two or three artifacts we recommend for a paper-based presenta-tion portfolio. A reviewer, rather than manually turning pages to locate a pertinent artifact, simply has to point and click to pull up a document or view a video. Reviewers can ignore those artifacts in which they have little interest.

**Increase Accessibility.** With a paper-based portfolio, a reviewer must have access to a VCR and monitor to watch a videotape of a teaching episode, a cassette recorder to listen to an audiotape of a presentation, and a computer to examine a PowerPoint presentation. These types of artifacts become far more accessible when the portfolio is in electronic form and can be viewed where and when the reviewer has access to a computer: in the office, on an airplane, or in a conference room immediately before an interview.

# Creation of Electronic Portfolios

The steps for assembling a professional portfolio described in Chapter 2 apply as well to the development of an electronic portfolio. However, if you intend to develop an electronic portfolio, there are two considerations you will want to keep in mind as you create and collect artifacts to document your competence.

## Save Artifacts Electronically

Creating an electronic presentation portfolio will be much easier if you are con-scientious about saving potential documents electronically. Most, if not all, of the paper-based products you create will be done on a computer. While you can save a copy of the final product on your computer hard drive, a computer crash or virus will destroy your work. A more reliable alternative is to save your work on either a CD or zip disk. You can create folders that correspond to the standards around which you plan to organize your portfolio. You would have ten folders, for instance, if you use the INTASC standards. As you create potential documents for your portfolio, they can be placed in the folder that corresponds to the appropriate standard.

## Document Your Experiences Electronically

As you proceed through your teacher education program or prepare for national board certification, keep in mind the unique opportunities that exist for documenting experiences electronically. Since video, audio, and digital photographs can easily be integrated into an electronic portfolio, you will want to record experiences or events that can later be included in your portfolio to document your competence or achievement of standards. This means, for example, recording videos of lessons you teach, audios of presentations you make, and digital photographs of bulletin boards you create. While you may not use all these artifacts in your presentation portfolio, the opportunity to include them is lost unless they are recorded in the appropriate format.

# Stages for Developing Electronic Portfolios

Creating an electronic portfolio involves two processes: portfolio development and multimedia development. The former is dealt with in detail in this book. Developing a multimedia project such as a portfolio can be described in four stages: Decide, Design, Develop, and Evaluate.[1]

## Decide

During the initial phase of multimedia project development, you need to determine the purpose of your portfolio and the needs of your potential audience. If your portfolio will be used during a checkpoint/transition point in a teacher education program, you may want to organize your artifacts around program requirements or standards. If you are seeking a teaching position, your portfolio might be organized around state teaching standards, the INTASC standards for beginning teachers, or standards appropriate for your particular discipline or content area. The National Board for Professional Teaching Standards has specific guidelines for the organization and structure of portfolios to be used when seeking national certification.

You also want to determine the availability of essential resources for the development of an electronic portfolio. Figure 3.1 provides a list of basic hardware

[1]Ivers, K., & Barron, A. E. (1998). *Multimedia projects in education.* Englewood, CO: Unlimited Libraries.

*The Computer*
A multimedia computer is best.
- RAM (Random Access Memory)—At least 256 MB, 512 MB is better.
- Processor—The faster the better.
- Hard Drive—At least 20 GB, more is better.
- Video Memory—At least 8 GB.
- Audio System—Standard card and speaker system should be fine.
- CD-ROM—The higher the speed, the better.
- Ports and Slots—At least two USB connectors.
- Modem—Faster is better.

*Peripherals*
- Scanner—A flatbed scanner is probably the most versatile.
- Digital Camera—The best you can afford.
- SCSI Drives—e.g., Iomega's Zip drive.
- CD-RW—Allows you to record on a CD.

**FIGURE 3.1**    Basic Hardware Requirements for Electronic Portfolio Development

requirements that will make the process of creating an electronic portfolio easier and more enjoyable.[2] This is not equipment you necessarily need to own; the items on the list are usually available at universities and school districts.

You should also assess your own knowledge and skills related to technology. The prospect of developing something as technologically complex as an electronic portfolio may be daunting if you feel you lack the necessary skills. This should not prevent you from proceeding, however. One option is to learn the required skills through formal coursework, workshops, or individual tutorials. The acquisition of these skills can be used to both develop your electronic portfolio and integrate technology into your teaching. A less desirable but perhaps more realistic short-term solution would be to locate someone who possesses the necessary skills to assist you in the development process.

## Design

The design phase involves determining the content of your portfolio and identifying and selecting the most appropriate software, storage, and presentation medium (e.g., computer hard drive, zip disk, CD-ROM, WWW server). The criteria you use in selecting artifacts for your electronic portfolio are the same we recommend for a paper-based portfolio and are described in Chapter 2. The most important consideration is that the artifacts document your abilities in the

[2]Kilbane, C., & Milman, N. (2003). *The digital teaching portfolio handbook: A how-to guide for educators.* Boston: Allyn and Bacon.

TaskStream (http://taskstream.com/pub/)
Kid Pix (The Learning Company, http://www.riverdeep.net)
PowerPoint (Microsoft, http://www.microsoft.com)
HyperStudio (Knowledge Adventure, http://www.HyperStudio.com)
Acrobat (Adobe, http://www.adobe.com)
e-Portfolio (Chalk & Wire, http://www.chalkandwire.com/eportfolio/)

**FIGURE 3.2**    Software Suggestions for Electronic Portfolio Development

professional standards you have selected. Just as in a paper-based portfolio, you will want to be selective, including artifacts tailored to the teaching position/certificate you are seeking.

One of the most important considerations when selecting software is its ability to create hypertext links between your artifacts and the standards around which you have organized your portfolio. Hypertext links allow the reader to navigate effortlessly between related artifacts, one of the great advantages electronic portfolios have over paper-based portfolios. Figure 3.2 presents a sampling of available and appropriate software for such a task.[3]

A very beneficial exercise during the design phase is to create a flowchart or storyboards. These are visual representations illustrating both the content of your portfolio and, in the case of a flowchart, the manner in which artifacts are linked or connected in your portfolio. For instance, you might link a unit of study with a digital photograph of a bulletin board and an individual lesson plan all placed under different standards. These kinds of design decisions are best made prior to the actual creation of your electronic portfolio.

## Develop

Once your artifacts have been selected and you have mapped out how they will be connected to the standards and, if appropriate, to each other, it is time to begin the actual development process. During this phase you will incorporate all your artifacts, whether they are text, digital photographs, audio, or video into a completed program stored on either a CD-ROM or zip disk.

In many cases, the experiences you documented in digital form will need some editing and/or revision prior to incorporating them into your final electronic portfolio. Video clips may need to be edited, text documents revised, digital photographs cropped, for example. Remember that the goal, as in a paper-based

[3]Kilbane, C., & Milman, N. (2003). *The digital teaching portfolio handbook: A how-to guide for educators.* Boston: Allyn and Bacon.

portfolio, is to showcase your best work as a professional. You will also, as in a paper-based portfolio, want to write a rationale for each artifact in which you describe the artifact, justify its placement under a particular standard, and discuss what the artifact says about your growing competence. Rationales are a critical characteristic of any well-developed professional portfolio.

As in a paper-based portfolio, you will also want to be creative and develop an electronic portfolio that is uniquely yours. The addition of graphics, animations, or audio will make your portfolio visually and auditorally appealing to reflect your unique and individual strengths and competencies. Some software programs include collections of clip art that you can incorporate into your portfolio. Numerous sites exist on the web where you can download and use graphics, animations, and audio files. Always read and check the permission statement and other restrictions that might apply to the individual use of these files.

## Evaluate

During the final phase of multimedia project development, you will evaluate both the content of your portfolio and the design of the multimedia format. The artifacts should reflect your best work as a growing or accomplished professional. The relationship between the artifacts and the standard under which they have been placed should be clear. As mentioned at the beginning of this chapter, an electronic portfolio allows you to document your competence in ways not possible in a paper-based portfolio. Take advantage of this opportunity and include artifacts that could not be presented in a paper-based format.

The multimedia aspects of your electronic portfolio should also be evaluated. Is your presentation clear, concise, and visually appealing? Do the graphics, animations, and other design features enhance or detract from the overall presentation? Is movement between and among standards and artifacts easily navigable? Remember that those doing the viewing will, in all likelihood, have far less technological competence than you, thus the overall program should be user friendly. We would suggest that you solicit friends and colleagues to evaluate your electronic portfolio and to provide you with suggestions for improvement.

It is always helpful to see completed examples of any project. Figure 3.3 provides the URLs for sample electronic portfolios of both preservice and inservice teachers available for review on the Internet.

Because of the time, expertise, and resources required to create and develop an electronic portfolio, you will not want to make frequent changes or revisions. Thus, it makes most sense to develop your electronic portfolio as a presentation portfolio. The suggestions we provide in Chapter 5 on the use of a portfolio at different stages of your career apply to any portfolio, regardless of format and structure.

Like most challenging projects, the greatest reward and learning come not at the time of project completion, but during the development process. Creating an

*Preservice Teacher Portfolios*
http://www.bsu.edu/web/mlfrownfelte/portfolio/frameset.html
http://www.bsu.edu/web/knkramer/index.html
http://durak.org/kathy/portfolio/
http://www.albion.edu/education/mcoatt/balbery/portfolio/
http://www.uwlax.edu/student/Efolio/Elementary/
http://www.portfolio.rimestimes.net/
http://homepages.wmich.edu/~v8vanhui/
http://www.kzoo.edu/pfolio/example/totten/

*Inservice Teacher Portfolios*
http://muskingum.edu/~jjohnson/edportfolio/index.html
http://www.mandia.com/kelly/portfolio.htm
http://www.cdli.ca/~delambe/index.html
http://www.wizzlewolf.com/ep.html

**FIGURE 3.3**    Websites Providing Examples of Electronic Portfolios

electronic portfolio can be a rewarding, valuable learning experience, albeit time-consuming and difficult. However, the rewards are potentially significant, both in terms of the completed product and the skills you acquire in development. The content of your electronic portfolio speaks to your competence as a professional, while the format demonstrates your technological knowledge and skill.

## TRY THIS

### Developing a Flowchart

Creating a flowchart or storyboard is a necessary initial step in the successful development of an electronic portfolio. A flowchart provides a visual representation illustrating the content of your portfolio and the manner in which you intend to connect or link the artifacts.

First you need to identify the standards around which you intend to build your electronic portfolio. For each standard, begin by selecting an artifact that documents your professional growth or work. Perhaps you have developed a unit of study on westward expansion and the Oregon Trail and decided to file it under Standard One. Begin your flowchart by placing the name of the artifact inside a box.

*Unit of Study*
*Oregon Trail*

Now consider the artifacts related to your unit that would more fully document your professional competence and growth. An electronic portfolio allows you to link these artifacts to your unit of study. Complete the flowchart for this particular artifact by connecting related documents to the unit of study.

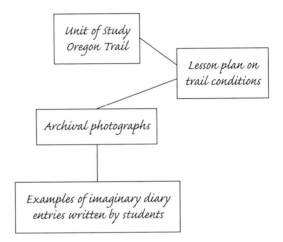

If you intend to create an electronic portfolio, the development of a flowchart is an important initial step in the planning process and should prove helpful as you begin the actual development process.

# 4

# Organization of Portfolios around Teaching Standards

## How to Use This Chapter

The art and science of teaching is a complex and challenging activity that cannot be totally and succinctly described by any set of goals, standards, or analysis of duties. However, for the purpose of charting and demonstrating professional growth through a portfolio, some system of categories is needed, imperfect though it may be. You are encouraged to select or develop your own set of standards or goals from the many available through universities, state departments of education, and national professional organizations. Indeed, your university program or school district may have a list of goals, competencies, or outcome statements that you may be asked to use as your standards for teaching. If not, refer to Appendix A for a list of organizations that have authored sets of teaching standards. Or, you may wish to adopt or adapt the set used as an example in this textbook.

For the purposes of providing a working example of a portfolio, we have chosen a set of standards or principles developed by the Chief State School Officers' Consortium on licensing, INTASC. The standards are chosen because they were developed by studying standards from many professional associations and the National Board for Professional Teaching Standards (NBPTS). These standards are a general or core set of expectations for all teaching, written in terms of performance and knowledge. Therefore, they have wide applicability. Furthermore, these standards have received wide acceptance and use.

If you choose to organize your portfolio around the INTASC standards, you will find this chapter handy. Each of the ten standards is explained and depicted in a real-life scenario. Then, you are shown a sample portfolio rationale page that could be used with artifacts to document each standard. Therefore, you will be able to read each standard, understand what it means, and picture it in practice.

If you are not using the INTASC standards but have adopted another set of standards instead, this chapter will also be useful to you. Exemplary teaching behaviors are somewhat universally understood. Therefore, the set of standards you have chosen will have concepts similar to the INTASC standards and, in some cases, the same wording. For example, standards offered by the NBPTS for early childhood teachers contain a standard called "Understanding Young Children." The concept of gaining and applying knowledge of child development is the specific teaching behavior outlined in this standard. It is essentially the same concept as INTASC Standard Two, "Knowledge of Human Development and Learning." Because Standard Two is described and depicted in this chapter, you will want to read that section carefully to gain insights into that area of teaching. Do this for all the standards in your set of goals. You can refer to Figure 1.1 in Chapter 1 and compare your standard statements to the INTASC standards. Then, return to this chapter and read the examples that apply to your teaching situation. Although the scenarios may not portray actual experiences you have had, they will help you picture opportunities for documenting your professional growth.

## How This Chapter Is Organized

Chapter 4 is organized in this manner:

1. *Statement of the Standard*
   In turn, each of the ten standards or principles for effective teaching as stated by INTASC is presented.

2. *Explanation of the Standard*
   A short explanation of the standard is provided to add clarity. If you are not using INTASC standards, this explanation of each standard will help you determine similarities and differences between your chosen goals and the ones described here.

3. *Teaching Scenario*
   Examples typical of preservice and inservice teachers' activities both inside and outside college classrooms are presented. Examples are used from four levels of teaching: early childhood, elementary, middle school, and secondary. The scenarios illustrate situations in which professional activities are indicators of achievement of the standards. Such illustrations will help you relate your set of standards, whether from INTASC or another source, to your everyday experiences as a preservice teacher.

4. *Sample Rationale Pages for Artifacts*

Following each scenario is a sample rationale page for artifacts that could document achieved competence in a particular standard. Writing rationale statements is typically the most difficult part of your portfolio development; therefore, you will want to pay close attention to them. You may want to use them as models for your own rationale statements in your portfolio. Therefore, all sample rationale pages in this book have been identified by shading and an icon.

Remember, all of the material presented in this chapter is for the purpose of example and not meant to imply any view of a single correct way to teach or document professional growth in a portfolio.

# Knowledge of Subject Matter

## Standard One

The teacher understands the central concepts, tools of inquiry, and structures of the discipline(s) he or she teaches and can create learning experiences that make these aspects of subject matter meaningful for students.

## Explanation of the Standard

Knowledge of subject matter is universally considered an essential attribute for effective teaching and successful learning. The most meaningful and lasting learning occurs when knowledge is constructed by individual students. The role of the teacher is to help learners build their own knowledge through acting on materials and engaging in meaningful experiences. To create these experiences, teachers must possess an in-depth understanding of major concepts, assumptions, debates, processes of inquiry, and ways of knowing that are central to the disciplines they teach.

Knowledge of subject matter also implies an understanding of inquiry used in various disciplines. Inquiry training lets students experience the same process actual scientists go through when attempting to explain a puzzling phenomenon. Employing methods such as inquiry training in the classroom allows teachers to engage learners in generating knowledge and testing hypotheses according to the methods of inquiry and standards of evidence used in the discipline.

In every classroom, it is critical that the teacher evaluate resources and curriculum materials for their comprehensiveness, accuracy, and usefulness for representing particular ideas and concepts. Subject matter knowledge would be essential for the selection and evaluation of curriculum materials and resources.

To illustrate "Knowledge of Subject Matter," the following scenario describes how a student in a social studies methods class developed a unit of study centered around a diary written by a 13-year-old girl.

## Teaching Scenario

Charlie is a junior education major enrolled in a course called "Teaching Social Studies in the Middle School." A requirement of the course is the development of a unit of study. Charlie has a particular interest in U.S. history, so he decides to do an eighth-grade unit on the Oregon Trail.

Charlie begins his work by reviewing how the topic is dealt with in a traditional social studies curriculum. He examines several eighth-grade social studies texts and finds that the Oregon Trail experience is covered very briefly. Charlie is also dissatisfied with the manner in which the subject is treated: primarily through names, dates, and facts. Charlie would like his students to gain an understanding and appreciation of what the four-month journey was like for those individuals and families who made the long and dangerous trip.

Charlie learned from his professor that, according to the research, children benefit most from forms of narrative history that involve the particular—that is, where a person or small group copes with a particular problem in a particular place at a particular time and under a particular set of circumstances. This type of historical material is most commonly found in original source materials such as journals, diaries, letters, biographies, and in historical fiction.

As a result of his knowledge, Charlie decides to focus his unit of study around a diary written during the overland crossing by a 13-year-old girl. The regular social studies textbook, rather than being the primary source of information, will become one of many secondary resource materials.

The unit is designed so that Charlie's students travel the Oregon Trail along with the young girl. They read her words describing the daily routine, the blazing heat, the lack of water, the river crossings, contact with Native Americans, and so forth. Charlie's students can share the joy of this young girl when she and her family finally reach Oregon.

Charlie lists the major concepts the unit will cover, designs appropriate corresponding instructional activities, and lists necessary materials. He describes in some detail how he plans to begin the unit and a culminating activity to provide closure.

Charlie is pleased with the finished product. Apparently the instructor is also pleased, because Charlie receives favorable comments. Charlie decides that his unit would be an excellent choice to include in his portfolio. A copy of his rationale page follows.

## SAMPLE RATIONALE PAGE

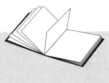

*Artifact for Standard One: Knowledge of Subject Matter*

*Name of Artifact:* Oregon Trail Unit
*Date:* October 2, XXXX
*Course:* EDE 306—Teaching of Social Studies in the Middle School
*Rationale:*

I have included this unit of study in my portfolio to document my knowledge of the subject matter. The topic of the unit is the Oregon Trail. The subject is primarily dealt with through the use of a diary of a young girl who made the crossing in 1849. Current research on how children best learn history indicates that using a primary source document such as a diary would be a particularly effective technique, since children best relate to historical events through some kind of narrative. Learning about the Oregon Trail experience through the words of someone close to their own age would be interesting and enjoyable for my students. This unit is historically accurate and is constructed in agreement with the current research on how to effectively teach history to children. I believe it documents my knowledge of the subject matter. From this experience, I have learned the importance of knowing the subject matter that I teach. In particular, I learned how to use a primary source document when teaching about historical events. My future lesson plans for social studies will include the use of such resources.

# Knowledge of Human Development and Learning

## Standard Two

The teacher understands how children learn and develop and can provide learning opportunities that support their intellectual, social, and personal development.

## Explanation of the Standard

A teacher working with a particular group of children or adolescents quickly realizes how each individual is unique. Differing personalities, learning abilities, interests, and skills make clear the wide variation in students of approximately the same age. And yet, in spite of wide differences, common characteristics unite students within an age group. Thus, although children and adolescents grow and develop at different rates and with varied abilities, there are predictable patterns and sequences to their development.

    Understanding these patterns, sequences, and stages of development is essential groundwork for a teacher making decisions about the content and methods of educating a group of students. Educational practice, to be effective, must be rooted in the rapidly advancing research and theory of human development and learning. Often such theory cannot be translated directly into teaching practice. However, when the teacher has a broad understanding of how people learn and develop, this knowledge can be useful in making logical hypotheses in how best to understand and thus respond to an individual student or group of students.

    As teachers test their hypotheses in the classroom, they must carefully observe the responses of students and the effects of their curricular choices. Rather than "covering material," teachers must evaluate the quality of the understanding of the content and the developmental appropriateness for the instructional strategies used. Thus, teachers gain knowledge from two sources about how students learn and develop: the fields of human development and psychology and their own observations of students and reflections about their teaching. The following scenario depicts how a college student uses a study of Piaget's theory of child development to demonstrate her competence in "Knowledge of Human Development and Learning."

## Teaching Scenario

Stacey is a sophomore elementary education major. As part of the General Education requirement, Stacey has taken a course in educational psychology. The works of many psychologists and learning theorists are dealt with in class (e.g., David Ausubel, Benjamin Bloom, Lawrence Kohlberg, Jean Piaget, Erik Erikson). Students are assigned to write a paper about the work and contributions to education of one person discussed in class. Stacey selects Jean Piaget as a subject for her paper.

Stacey begins the paper by presenting background information on Piaget. She reports on his early studies in biology and how he became interested in child development. She discusses the principal concepts of Piaget's theory: schemata, assimilation, accommodation, and equilibration. The bulk of the paper, however, discusses Piaget's four stages of cognitive development: sensorimotor, preoperational, concrete operational, and formal operational. She states that Piaget believed that all children pass through these stages in order, and no child can skip a stage, although different children pass through the stages at somewhat different rates.

Stacey describes the approximate age of children at each stage of development. She also details the cognitive capabilities of children at any one stage. For instance, at the preoperational stage, Stacey notes that children can now arrange things in order according to one attribute such as size or weight. This means that children can line up sticks from smallest to largest. Stacey also lists learning activities commonly used in elementary classrooms that illustrate this ability. Stacey concludes her paper by summarizing criticisms and revisions of Piaget's theory.

Stacey's professor returns the paper with favorable comments. She is impressed with Stacey's research, her writing skills, and her ability to relate Piaget's theory to classroom instruction. She feels the paper indicates that Stacey has a sound understanding of both Piaget's work and his contributions to educational practice. Because of her interest in the subject and the professor's positive evaluation, Stacey decides to include this paper in her portfolio. Her rationale page is shown here.

## SAMPLE RATIONALE PAGE

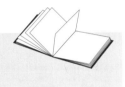

*Artifact for Standard Two: Knowledge of Human Development and Learning*

*Name of Artifact:* Research Paper on Jean Piaget
*Date:* October 23, XXXX
*Course:* PSY 208—Educational Psychology
*Rationale:*

To document my knowledge of human development, I have selected a research paper I wrote for a class in educational psychology. The subject of the paper was Jean Piaget. I described his four stages of cognitive development and common tasks children at each stage can accomplish. I also described classroom activities that illustrate a child's cognitive ability. I concluded the paper by discussing criticisms of Piaget's theory. I have also included with this paper the positive comments my professor made concerning my work. The research I conducted for this paper and my ability to relate Piaget's work to classroom practice demonstrate my knowledge of child development. Piaget's work has greatly influenced my outlook on child development. As I make plans for learning opportunities for my students in my future classes, I will continue to observe children closely and reflect Piagetian principles in my teaching.

# Adapting Instruction for Individual Needs

## Standard Three

The teacher understands how students differ in their approaches to learning and creates instructional opportunities that are adapted to diverse learners.

## Explanation of the Standard

There are broad differences in students and the skills they bring to the learning environment. These differences include varied learning styles, diverse cultural backgrounds, and exceptionality in learning. The effective teacher understands how children differ in their development and approaches to learning and is able to adapt strategies and environments to meet specific needs of children. Therefore, a major role of the teacher is to assess each student's developmental levels and abilities in all areas and match learning environments and experiences appropriately. To fulfill this role, a teacher must be an astute observer of students and a professional who can use observational data to diagnose, guide, and instruct. Further, the teacher must design instruction that helps use students' strengths as the basis for their growth. In this classroom, students are valued for their uniqueness and they learn to respect this in one another. The classroom environment then becomes a learning community in which individual differences are respected.

As students' differences become clear, the teacher might adjust task assignments, time allowed, circumstances for work, and communication and response modes for individual students. In some instances, the teacher will participate in and assist other professionals in family-centered assessment and in the development and implementation of individualized plans for children with special developmental and learning needs. To further explain how instruction can be adapted to individual needs, the following scenario describes how a student teacher worked with students with special needs to help them complete a class assignment.

## Teaching Scenario

Jess is a student teacher in Mr. Addlestein's tenth-grade English class. At the beginning of the semester, he has a conference with Mr. Addlestein and discovers that there are three students with disabilities in his class, and a fourth student is learning English as a second language (ESL). Jess begins to think about ways in which he can adapt instruction to meet the needs of all students in this class.

During a unit on biographies and autobiographies, Jess decides to use the writing process to have all students write their own autobiographies. He issues written contracts and conducts conferences with each student to make a tentative time line for completing each step of the writing process. The four students are offered extra help. At least two extra conferences are planned, and each student is assigned a peer tutor. All students are encouraged to use childhood photographs, magazine pictures, newspaper articles and headlines, or their own creative artwork to help express their ideas for writing the autobiography. Jess feels that this will especially help the students make clear what they want to say in their autobiographies.

Jess decides to include this information in his portfolio for Standard Three. In the tabbed section, he includes a copy of the written contracts made with one of the four special needs students, along with his anecdotal notes made during writing conferences. He also includes a copy of the autobiography written by this student. In front of all this, he inserts a rationale page similar to the following example.

## SAMPLE RATIONALE PAGE

*Artifact for Standard Three: Adapting Instruction for Individual Needs*

*Name of Artifact:* Results of Writing Process with Students Having Special Needs

*Date:* September 18, XXXX

*Course:* EDE 461—Student Teaching

*Rationale:*

During my student teaching, I learned that my class included four students with special needs, including one who is learning English as a Second Language. To ensure that these students could successfully complete a writing assignment, I needed to adapt my plans to their needs. Therefore, I wrote contracts with them that allowed for extra time, if needed, and planned at least two extra writing conferences. A sample contract and the conference notes on one student are included in this section. During those conferences, I asked this ESL student to bring pictures from magazines and newspapers that he especially liked and reminded him of home. We discussed these, and I taught him several new words this way. Editing and revising were encouraged through his specially assigned peer tutor as well as during our conferences. My anecdotal notes, which I include here, were taken during our writing conferences and show the progress he made over the course of the assignment. His end product was successful and shows evidence of growth. It is also included in this section.

I feel these documents show my ability to create a learning experience that would meet the special needs of a student. I knew that the plans I made for most of the rest of the class would not allow this student to have success with the assignment. Therefore, I tailored the assignment so that he could be successful and grow intellectually as well as socially. By working with these four students, I learned about the need for this type of adaptation when teaching. I believe that I will teach differently as a result of this experience because I now know that meeting individual needs does not just happen; I must continually assess my students and provide appropriate environments for them.

# Multiple Instructional Strategies

## Standard Four

The teacher understands and uses a variety of instructional strategies to encourage students' development of critical thinking, problem solving, and performance skills.

## Explanation of the Standard

Teachers deal daily with many complexities, including differences among their students in terms of abilities, attitudes, and learning preferences. For these widely varying students, there are multiple goals and objectives to be met, including those dealing with content, basic skills, problem solving, attitudes, dispositions, and critical thinking skills. It is clear that no routine or "pet" teaching approach can effectively meet all of these needs. Effective teachers draw from a wide repertoire of instructional strategies and models, adjusting their choices to meet their intended objectives and the needs of particular students.

There are many instances in which the most efficient and effective way to teach certain kinds of knowledge is through expository teaching or teacher-directed, step-by-step learning. In such cases, direct instruction, presentations, and skills practice are appropriate. However, there are many other times when methods that appear time consuming yield the greatest results in the long run. When students are given the time and materials to be active investigators, they are able to construct a basic framework of knowledge within which to expand their understanding.

Learning for understanding often requires experimentation, problem solving, collaboration, and manipulation of physical objects. Therefore, teachers need models of teaching that include inquiry learning, cooperative learning, concept attainment, and class discussions. These models have as a goal the formation of cognitive structures including concepts, generalizations, dispositions, and understandings rather than simple attainment of specific facts or mastery of discrete skills. As teachers understand the wide variety of instructional strategies available, they will be better able to choose and combine them to integrate affective and cognitive development and to educate for understanding, both of content and of self. Such understandings are exemplified in the example that follows. This is an actual university classroom scenario in which the preservice teacher was investigating ways to teach important concepts to preschoolers.

## Teaching Scenario

Erica is an undergraduate enrolled in a course dealing with the content and methods of teaching mathematics in early childhood classrooms. Erica is a member of a small group of students assigned to do an in-depth investigation of developmentally appropriate ways to teach geometric shapes and spatial concepts to children ages 3 to 6 (preschool). Erica's group is to present its findings to the total class.

Very early into the research, Erica and her fellow students realize that young children learn geometric shapes and spatial concepts best by actively manipulating a wide variety of materials designed to provide extensive and active practice with these concepts. Erica's group begins gathering commercially made manipulatives. The group members also make several teaching materials and games, including bingo, shape twister, a spatial obstacle course, and flannel board story figures that teach spatial and shape concepts. Finally, Erica's group finds pieces of children's literature as well as computer programs appropriate for teaching children geometric shapes and spatial concepts.

Erica and her group realize that the use of manipulatives by themselves is not enough; they must be accompanied by instructional strategies that promote active inquiry learning. Their research shows them that the teacher facilitates the learning by providing children with opportunities to explore the materials. The teacher guides them through their play by using inductive questioning, encouraging cooperative problem solving, and modeling appropriate vocabulary for new concepts.

To reinforce their learning of these instructional strategies, Erica and her team members visit a local preschool and observe the teachers. They take notes on the types of questions the teachers ask as children experiment with manipulatives. These questions enable the children to induce concepts on their own; thus, they are actively constructing their own knowledge. Erica and her teammates also pay close attention to the way in which the teachers model problem solving for the youngsters and the way in which they explain new concepts and vocabulary. All of this information is included in an observation log, so that Erica and the rest of the group can outline specific instructional strategies to be used with their manipulatives.

These teaching strategies and the materials that accompany them are presented to the total class. Erica's group decides to present these materials through learning centers, much the way materials would be organized for young children. Each set of materials contains a description of the types of questions to ask while the children are playing and the types of problems to ask children to solve.

Erica is proud of what she has learned and the teaching materials she has designed and collected. She decides to document this work for her portfolio by taking pictures of the learning stations on the day of the class presentation. She also prepares descriptions and sketches of the teacher-made materials she designed along with the descriptions of teaching strategies for active inquiry learning. Finally, Erica prepares a bibliography of the children's literature, computer software, and resource books her group identified. All of this goes into her portfolio, and Erica is careful to give credit to her fellow group members where appropriate. She writes the following rationale statement for these documents.

*SAMPLE RATIONALE PAGE*

*Artifact for Standard Four: Multiple Instructional Strategies*

*Name of Artifact:* Teaching Math Concepts to
        Preschool Children
*Date:* November 12, XXXX
*Course:* ECE 315—Math Content and Methods in Early Childhood
*Rationale:*

In fulfilling a class assignment to investigate methods and materials used to teach geometric and spatial concepts, I have demonstrated that I can identify instructional strategies that promote inquiry learning. With three peers, I investigated ways to question students so that they learn inductively as well as ways to model problem solving and concept development. This investigation took place in a preschool classroom in which we observed exemplary teachers using these teaching strategies. I found developmentally appropriate math materials that are commercially available and would actively engage students. I also demonstrated my ability to design teacher-made math materials that are versatile, durable, attractive, and age appropriate. These materials were designed to be used by small groups of students and would invite cooperative, hands-on learning. In addition, I was able to find computer programs and pieces of children's literature to help teach the concepts under consideration.

In presenting these strategies and materials to my class, I prepared clear, understandable descriptions of the types of questions and modeling to use when teaching these concepts through inquiry learning. In addition, I prepared concise directions for using the learning materials. To document my abilities, I have included pictures of the materials, narratives that describe them and their accompanying teaching strategies, the observation log that documents investigation, and a bibliography of materials that the other group members and I identified to teach the specified math concepts. I have learned how important it is to use a variety of strategies when teaching. These instructional strategies will continue to be useful for me as I write new lesson plans for my future students.

# Classroom Motivation and Management

## Standard Five

The teacher uses an understanding of individual and group motivation and behavior to create a learning environment that encourages positive social interaction, active engagement in learning, and self-motivation.

## Explanation of the Standard

Effective teachers work in many ways to build positive classroom interactions. These teachers recognize that involving students in this endeavor not only promotes growth in personal and social responsibility but also enhances the development of democratic and social values. Group rapport is enhanced as students and teachers work cooperatively to establish classroom norms and rules. Teaching and modeling effective problem-solving techniques such as conflict resolution provide motivation for learning, positive social interaction among children, and positive self-esteem for all. Thus, the effective teacher strives to create a learning community that fosters group decision making, collaboration, individual responsibility, and self-directed learning.

Teachers interested in building and sustaining a positive learning climate are aware of the range of behavioral phenomena confronting them. They recognize that there are situations in which the teacher will be confronted by students who are unable to function within the parameters established by the group. In these instances, teachers must rely upon their knowledge of the principles and strategies of behavior management and issues related to all aspects of motivation. As reflective practitioners, teachers use this knowledge of theory, along with their classroom experiences, to construct an ever-evolving student motivation and management philosophy. This philosophy is specific enough to guide classroom actions yet flexible enough to accommodate the individual needs of students. Therefore, effective classroom managers understand the need to be able to define problems, identify alternatives, choose a course of action and a plan for implementation, and consider the possible consequences of a given action. The teaching scenario that follows shows how a preservice teacher was able to assess his ability to create a positive learning environment and modify his own teaching behaviors to improve the climate of his classroom.

## Teaching Scenario

While enrolled in an early field experience class, Mikhail has the opportunity to spend a few hours every week in a daycare classroom working with children ages 3 to 5. Mikhail soon realizes that these young children can be very impetuous and need a great deal of support from teachers in developing self-control and learning how to function in a group.

The college instructor in the class addresses "Promoting Positive Guidance" as one of her seminar topics. In class, Mikhail and his classmates practice phrasing requests and directions to young children in a positive, encouraging way that would invite the children's cooperation and teach them problem-solving and negotiating skills. Mikhail values this instruction a great deal because he realizes that he has a tendency to be directive and often negative with children, using a great many "don'ts." Mikhail decides to systematically practice these positive guidance techniques in the classroom with children.

He asks a fellow classmate who is doing field work with him at the daycare center to observe and record any negative, discouraging, or demanding comments that he makes to the children. After receiving her observations, Mikhail reflects on how he could have communicated those same requests to the children in a positive, encouraging way. Gradually, Mikhail finds he is gaining in his ability to spontaneously use positive verbal guidance. He is also becoming more likely to invite problem solving rather than solve problems through correcting children.

Mikhail is proud of this growth; he can see how his behavior is resulting in a much better rapport with these children and is helping to create a more positive social climate. Mikhail decides to document this work. He includes in his portfolio a videotape of his interactions with the group, anecdotal records of his growth based on the observations of his classmate, and the following rationale page.

## SAMPLE RATIONALE PAGE

*Artifact for Standard Five: Classroom Motivation and Management*

*Name of Artifact:* Evidence of Positive Verbal Guidance
*Date:* March 4, XXXX
*Course:* ECE 203—Field Experiences with Young Children
*Rationale:*

I have chosen to use two documents that indicate the growth I have attained in understanding how to create a positive learning environment with very young children. The first is a set of anecdotal records of interactions I had in a classroom of 3- to 5-year-olds and my reflections on the outcomes of those interactions. The anecdotal records show growth in my ability to formulate positive, encouraging requests and responses to children. The second is a videotape of myself near the end of the field experience showing informal conversations with children and a teacher-directed activity. In this videotape, I demonstrate my ability to gain children's cooperation by the way I speak with them. I also demonstrate how I help the children solve problems with their peers, encouraging cooperation rather than taking over the situation. The strategies I am employing lead to positive social interaction and positive individual and group motivation. I am particularly proud of my professional growth as a result of this experience. I had never before realized the importance of phrasing requests and directions in a positive manner. My ability to motivate children and manage my future classroom has been greatly enhanced.

## Communication Skills

### Standard Six

The teacher uses knowledge of effective verbal, nonverbal, and media communication techniques to foster active inquiry, collaboration, and supportive interaction in the classroom.

## Explanation of the Standard

Much of teaching is about sending and receiving messages. Carefully planned and skillfully delivered messages can issue invitations to students that school is a place to share ideas, investigate, create, and collaborate with others. School can be a place to be understood as well as a place to gain understanding. But without intentional considerations and planning, the messages actually received by the students can be conflicting, confusing, or discouraging. For this reason, teachers need to monitor their personal verbal and nonverbal communication so it is characterized by clarity, organization, enthusiasm, and sensitivity. Teachers' oral and written communications need to be models of appropriate grammar, content, and syntax. Effective teachers consistently use active listening skills as well. These include the use of paraphrasing, perception checking, and clarifying questions.

Environments and resources, as well as people, send messages. The physical environment of a classroom can communicate to students many things. Bright, cheerful, colorful environments are likely to set expectations that this is a happy, interesting place to be. Classrooms where all of the students have work displayed is likely to communicate that all the children share this room and all are valued. When materials that are frequently used are stored so they are easily accessible, students learn that they can be independent in this classroom. The condition and organization of materials also communicate the importance the teacher attaches to the work that is done with those materials. Part of the effective teacher's role, therefore, is to select, adapt, and create a physical environment and a broad range of instructional resources that engage the students in exciting learning and that send the messages intended.

Effective teachers also recognize the increasing importance of technology as a tool for student learning and as a major communication resource to be developed. Technological media, classroom environment, and the teacher's verbal and nonverbal communication should all work together to send the students clear and consistent messages about classroom expectations, goals, and challenges. The following scenario describes how one student teacher came to appreciate the importance of one of these aspects of effective communication: giving clear verbal directions.

## Teaching Scenario

Before her student teaching experience in a kindergarten classroom, Nicole had not really considered the importance of lesson clarity. However, Nicole's first assignment with this class, teaching a game, brings the need for clarity home emphatically. Nicole's first direction for the game is for the children to get into a "u-shaped circle." The children know what a circle is, and most know what a "u" is. But they do not understand the term "u-shaped circle." As the children struggle to comply, Nicole keeps repeating this one directive. It is fully ten minutes before the intended semicircle is achieved. Unfortunately, it is not achieved without the cooperating teacher's stepping in and physically placing the children. Nicole realizes after that experience that students need unambiguous, specific directions and that these are not always easy to formulate.

Nicole thinks that this need for clarity is unique to very young children until she reflects on instances in college courses in which she has been frustrated by vague, indefinite assignments and activity directions. Nicole determines that for all her future lessons, she will strive for clarity in every instruction as well as in presentations of information.

Nicole's greatest challenge in lesson clarity comes when planning a cooperative learning activity that requires small groups of children to collaborate while assembling a terrarium. Nicole knows the result depends on the children's fully understanding the steps to the procedure and their roles in the activity. She plans with clarity as her goal.

Later, in watching a videotape of the children collaborating to make terraria, Nicole reflects on how far she has come since the day she taught that first game. In spite of the high level of activity, the need for cooperation, the potential for messiness, and the many steps to the procedure, the terrarium lesson is a huge success. Nicole is eager to portray in her portfolio her growth in this skill of lesson clarity. The following is a copy of her rationale page.

## SAMPLE RATIONALE PAGE

*Artifact for Standard Six: Communication Skills*

*Name of Artifact:* Video Showing Lesson Clarity
*Date:* December 6, XXXX
*Course:* EDE 461—Student Teaching
*Rationale:*

   I have included a lesson plan and a video of the same lesson in my portfolio to document how I achieved lesson clarity by utilizing effective verbal communication techniques. I have highlighted aspects of my lesson plan that indicate the techniques I used to achieve clarity and foster productive, active learning and collaboration. In this lesson, I planned for lesson clarity in a variety of ways. In the beginning, I demonstrated and discussed the entire process of terrarium construction. Later, when the students were in their carefully planned, heterogeneous learning groups, I reviewed the steps again using a picture and word chart to which they could refer. We also discussed the various jobs that could be shared among the group members and the value of allowing everyone to help. However, rather than assigning jobs, I allowed the groups to negotiate the assignment of these jobs. As my video shows, the children were successful in following directions and did an excellent job of sharing responsibilities. With this project, I gained first-hand knowledge about lesson clarity. The results were encouraging; it was apparent that my careful planning for clear communication helped facilitate my students' active engagement and cooperative learning. I have decided that communication skills will be a goal for all of my lesson plans.

# Instructional Planning Skills

## Standard Seven

The teacher plans instruction based on knowledge of subject matter, students, the community, and curriculum goals.

## Explanation of the Standard

An effective teacher plans learning experiences based on a set of diverse factors, each of which influences the outcome of student learning. First, the subject matter is considered. It is important that the teacher have a thorough knowledge of the composition of the subject being taught as well as an understanding of teaching methods that are unique to that subject. Second, the individual needs of learners are of utmost importance. Teachers need to be able to create short-range and long-term plans that are linked to student needs yet be ready to respond to unanticipated classroom events and adapt those plans to ensure student progress and motivation. Third, community needs and resources are a factor in planning lessons. Each community is unique in its citizens' consensus about what is important for its children to know. As public educators, teachers need to be sensitive to these beliefs and reflect on them when making plans. Fourth, curriculum goals are important. These goals give the teacher direction in making plans. Curriculum goals have a variety of sources: Many are provided by school districts and the local community; others are created by the teacher.

As teachers engage in both long-term and short-term planning, they must be flexible enough to consider these contexts: subject matter, local school district goals, current educational issues, legal issues, family and community considerations, public policies, and community resources. Tying all these together are the interests, needs, and aptitudes of each of the students being taught. While in the classroom, teachers need to be reflective of their current practice and be open to adjustments and revisions that become necessary in working with a diverse group of students. This self-reflection is evident in the teaching scenario that follows.

## Teaching Scenario

Pepita, a newly tenured fourth-grade teacher in a small rural school district, is in the process of updating her teaching portfolio. In searching for examples to document this standard, she reflects on lessons that demonstrate how she addressed the diverse needs of students through school curriculum goals and community-based resources. She has chosen an interdisciplinary unit that embraces the context of her community and school and teaches concepts of appreciating one's local heritage and understanding the uniqueness of regional cultures.

Pepita introduced the unit by asking students to examine several old family patchwork quilts. Discussions about the quilts were encouraged, and a KWL chart was created to further activate students' prior knowledge and assess students' levels of interest. In an effort to extend students' understanding of heritage and treasured memorabilia, she read *The Patchwork Quilt* by Valerie Flournoy. Students were then invited to select additional readings from a variety of quality children's literature highlighting the significance of quilts. These literary interactions and related responses were designed to help students create an understanding of the importance of the art of quilting as it relates to themselves and their community. Throughout the week, Pepita proceeded to extend student learning across disciplines as the class created a historic timeline of local quilt making from its inception to modern day techniques. Mathematical standards were addressed as students investigated patchwork quilt patterns and designed quilt puzzles for first-grade students. Students' investigations and comparisons of machines from needles and scissors to modern-day quilting machines connected to the science and technology standards. Students applied history and consumer science standards as they prepared cloth patches for the quilt top. Two classroom parents joined Pepita in assisting students as they used the traditional needle technique to assemble the fabric into one piece. The quilting process was completed by a local crafter who visited the classroom and demonstrated the art of modern-day quilting by applying the batting and backing using a quilting machine. To culminate the unit, students participated in a performance assessment task. Each child helped create an oral history that involved a videotaped interview of a well-known quilt maker. The activity and assessment included preparing for and conducting the interview, selecting and completing written responses, and designing a portrait of the quilt maker. Pepita created a partnership with the region's historical society that led to a display of the students' work at the annual local cultural arts festival where students met with local residents and discussed their work and quilt making.

## SAMPLE RATIONALE PAGE

*Artifact for Standard Seven: Instructional Planning Skills*

*Name of Artifact:* Interdisciplinary Cultural Heritage Unit
*Date:* April 12, XXXX
*Rationale:*

   The artifact I chose to use in documenting my instructional planning skills is an interdisciplinary unit on cultural heritage. I have included the unit goals and objectives, an outline of the daily lessons, samples of students' written responses, the videotape completed during the Oral History Project, and a class album compiled by the students with my guidance. This album includes photographs with descriptors showing the students involved in the creation of the math puzzles, sewing their individual quilt patches, interacting with the various community crafters, and participating in oral history displays at the local cultural arts festival. This study integrated the subject areas of literature, written composition, mathematics, science, social studies, and consumer science.

I filed this unit plan under Standard Seven because it clearly demonstrates my ability to plan, deliver, and adjust instruction based on the knowledge of subject, students, community, and curriculum goals. The extensive bibliography illustrates how students' interactions with both the related narrative and expository literature demanded provision of a greater quantity of reading materials than my original resources. Written reflections contained in my lesson plans prove how I monitored student interactions and performance and adapted accordingly. Through analyses of the variety and quality of the students' responses to their readings, I was able to confirm their understanding of the importance of the art of quilting as it relates to themselves and their community. As I reflect upon the entire unit, I believe evidence contained in the students' research, historic time lines, patterning investigations, designed quilt puzzles, and related writings attest to the connections students made to the content standards and regional heritage. I found that both the students' involvement in the festival and the partnership I developed with our region's historical society have served to further strengthen the connections between our school and community. This experience has encouraged me to continue in the future to find other ways to plan instruction that incorporates my knowledge of content, individual students' needs, as well as community and curriculum goals to create meaningful learning experiences for all students.

# Assessment of Student Learning

## Standard Eight

The teacher understands and uses formal and informal assessment strategies to ensure the continuous intellectual, social, and physical development of the learner.

## Explanation of Standard

The purpose of assessment is to assist students, teachers, schools, parents, and caregivers in recognizing what students have learned and to identify areas in which students need improvement. Teachers gather, synthesize, and evaluate many different types of information about their students to make effective decisions about instruction.

Traditional assessment has been based on specific information that students acquire. Observations, tests on content, and standardized tests are examples of traditional evaluative measures that provide indicators that suggest learning has taken place. These traditional measures, however, may tell little about the depth of knowledge in relation to solving real-life problems. New approaches to assessment have tried to address this need by focusing on performance samples in which students demonstrate that they can perform a task such as giving a speech, playing an instrument, or writing a story. Some of these tasks are called alternative assessments because they take place in a contrived context. They are an improvised or created "alternative" to a real-life problem-solving situation. In contrast, other performance tasks are authentic assessments because students demonstrate learning in a real-life setting. For example, a student might be asked to give a speech while running for school office. If the student wants to be elected, the speech must be convincing enough to accomplish this. This type of authentic assessment measures not only the student's ability to effectively demonstrate skills or solve problems but also his or her ability to assume responsibility for directing his or her own learning. Because of the benefits of using a variety of assessment strategies, many teachers are helping students to organize their work samples into portfolios. This approach to assessment relies on work samples and performance tasks that reflect the academic growth of the student over time. A student portfolio should include a variety of both authentic and alternative assessment samples. More specifically, teachers evaluate items such as learning logs, journals, criterion-referenced tests, observations, peer evaluations and self-evaluations, homework, and group projects. Whatever type of assessment is used, each should reflect the following three qualities: The assessment should be as reliable as possible. This means that the assessment should provide dependable, consistent results. In addition, the assessment strategies used by the teacher should be valid. In other words, the teacher should make sure that the assessment strategy measures what it claims to measure. Finally, the strategies should be fair, impartial, and unbiased.

The following scenario shows how a field experience student and a cooperating teacher gather, synthesize, and evaluate different types of assessment information in order to direct instruction.

## Teaching Scenario

Deidre is an education major enrolled in a field experience course. She has the opportunity to spend several hours a week in a language arts class at a middle school. The school has recently adopted the concept of portfolios and now directs its efforts to collecting alternative and authentic assessment measures to evaluate student writing.

At first, Deidre observes the teacher, students, and their interaction during writing lessons. She takes notes on student reaction to the lesson and lists various writing activities the students will be working on in the coming weeks.

Her supervising teacher encourages her to take part in the assessment of the student writing process. More specifically, she suggests that Deidre focus on the writing development of one particular student. The district's annual writing assessment project takes place over several days, follows the writing process approach, and results in a final draft. The student that Deidre selected not only has completed this writing task but also has written a persuasive speech in hopes that she will be elected secretary of the student council.

Deidre begins to notice a number of activities that could be included in this student's portfolio to assess progress in writing. Deidre collects anecdotal records of the student's progress during both of these writing projects. She is invited to observe writing conferences as well as read journal and learning-log entries.

Deidre is pleased that she has had the opportunity to observe and participate in this assessment project. She has collected several samples of different types of assessment and documented all of her observations. She begins to confer with her cooperating teacher to assess the student's writing progress in the last weeks. The first draft, the rewrite, and the final draft are sequenced to show progressive improvement. Anecdotal records and student comments in the learning log and journal entries reflect progress the student has made. With the permission of the cooperating teacher and the student, samples of this go into Deidre's portfolio. She is careful to delete the student's name and other forms of identification.

## SAMPLE RATIONALE PAGE

*Artifact for Standard Eight: Assessment of Student Learning*

*Name of Artifact:* Authentic and Alternative Assessments
of a Seventh-Grade Writer
*Date:* January 2, XXXX
*Course:* EDE 202—Field Experience
*Rationale:*

The artifacts provided in this section show the material that my cooperating teacher and I gathered in my effort to evaluate one student's writing. I recognized the writing task as a form of alternative assessment and chose to include developmental samples of this student's writing in my portfolio for Standard Eight.

I also included the draft and final copy of a persuasive speech prepared by the student, because this is an example of authentic assessment. The student's learning log revealed her knowledge of the writing process and her strengths and weaknesses. Journal entries reflected the enjoyment she derives from writing. I have read the student's writing, observed the writing process, watched presentations, reflected on the self-evaluations and peer evaluations, and reviewed homework. As a result, I have collected a record of this student's growth and development in writing. My cooperating teacher and I have gathered all the necessary samples to make a reliable, valid, unbiased evaluation of the student's writing. This information will be used to make effective decisions about future instruction. I have included my evaluation of this student's progress as well as her portfolio work samples because they show my ability to synthesize information about a student from a variety of sources of data. This experience truly taught me the importance of assessment. I was able to make appropriate instructional decisions about this student's writing, and that was quite exciting for me. This kind of ongoing assessment will be part of my teaching and will drive the kinds of strategies that I plan to use and type of classroom environment that I will provide.

# Professional Commitment and Responsibility

### Standard Nine

The teacher is a reflective practitioner who continually evaluates the effects of his or her choices and actions on others (students, parents, and other professionals in the learning community) and who actively seeks opportunities to grow professionally.

### Explanation of the Standard

A good teacher is one who has the ability to learn as much from the students as they learn from him or her. In an effort to match instruction to the needs of students, this teacher spends much time evaluating the implications of his or her teaching decisions in the classroom. This is the mark of a reflective practitioner. Such self-reflection leads to greater knowledge about the students, about the subject being taught, and about the act of teaching.

Self-reflection also takes place in considering the teacher's relationships with parents and educational professionals. The responsibilities of educators in a democratic society include that of working with a community of concerned individuals who rally around one central goal—educating children. Children learn much from their experiences within their families and the outside world. Recognizing these facts, the teacher must cultivate strong relationships with parents as well as with educational professionals, constantly reevaluating the effects of his or her decisions on all who are involved with the education of the students.

This constant evaluation of choices extends itself outside the classroom. Indeed, a teaching professional is one who has a need for continuing education. Certification is only the first step in a long process of continual development as a professional. Growing professionally means learning new ways to make lesson plans, understand subject matter more thoroughly, and manage a classroom, among hundreds of other skills. But true professionals need more than technical teaching skills. They must also have the ability to constantly self-evaluate and act critically. New ideas together with classroom experience form a stronger theoretical base from which the teacher works, allowing for more effective decision making in the classroom. Thus, it is crucial that teachers seek opportunities for professional growth and place new ideas within the theoretical framework that already exists in their classrooms.

The role of the reflective practitioner is demonstrated in the following scenario of Mary, an elementary preservice teacher. Note how Mary utilizes the skills of reflection and critical decision making in order to meet the needs of her students and to engage in professional growth with colleagues.

### Teaching Scenario

Mary, a preservice teacher, is completing her student teaching experience at Green Valley Elementary School. One student in her third-grade class, Michael, has been diagnosed with several emotional problems, which are affecting his academic work. While teaching this class, Mary is constantly challenged to meet this child's needs. She keeps a journal in which she records her daily activities while student teaching as well as her thoughts and reactions to classroom life. In this journal, she makes several entries about Michael's responses to her teaching decisions, making sure to keep his identity anonymous. She realizes that she would like to know more about how to help Michael succeed. She makes an appointment with the school psychologist, Dr. Rose, to discuss this. Dr. Rose makes several suggestions, which Mary documents in her journal. Mary asks her cooperating teacher if she may schedule a conference with Michael's parents to share ideas and learn more about how his behavior at home may be affecting his schoolwork. His parents, impressed with her professionalism, wrote her a note praising her dedication to helping their son. In addition, Mary checks out several books on the subject of emotional disabilities in the classroom and makes note of some of the suggestions outlined there. At the university, Mary leads a discussion in her student-teaching seminar on this subject, based on what she has learned in her reading. She creates a handout of suggestions and shares this with her classmates.

Mary decides to document Standard Nine with evidence of her experiences. She inserts the journal entries, the thank-you note from the parents, the bibliography of books on the subject, and the handout from the seminar into her portfolio. Her rationale page follows.

## SAMPLE RATIONALE PAGE

*Artifact for Standard Nine: Professional Commitment and Responsibility*

*Name of Artifact:* Collection of Documents on Emotional
     Disabilities in School
*Date:* May 21, XXXX
*Course:* EDU 410—Student Teaching
*Rationale:*
     My student-teaching experience presented me with a challenge. I worked with a little boy who was experiencing emotional difficulties that prevented him from succeeding in the classroom. I felt it was important for me to learn more about what I could do to help improve his classroom experiences, so I sought additional information. A visit with the school psychologist, a conference with the parents, and the reading of several books on the subject helped to add to my knowledge of how to teach this youngster and others like him. I shared this information in a seminar discussion with my classmates and found that many of them had the same challenges. We were able to share more ideas as the discussion progressed. I gave them a handout I prepared, outlining several teaching suggestions learned from my investigation of this problem. This handout is included as documentation of this standard.
     In addition, I have included my journal entries, which outline some of the questions I had about working with this child as well as some of the things I learned during

*(continued)*

*SAMPLE RATIONALE PAGE (continued)*

my discussions with the school psychologist. A thank-you note the parents wrote after our conference is included because it shows my commitment to building strong relationships with the family. Finally, a bibliography of books on emotional disabilities is included because it shows the research that I did to improve my knowledge of the subject. Perhaps the most important thing that I learned from this experience is that as a teacher, I will never stop reflecting and learning. I plan to continue learning more about emotional disabilities such as those this child had; but more importantly, I plan to continue learning more about this profession in general.

# Partnerships

### Standard Ten

The teacher fosters relationships with school colleagues, parents, and agencies in the larger community to support students' learning and well-being.

### Explanation of the Standard

Effective teachers engage in a variety of experiences within and beyond the school that promote a spirit of collaboration, collegiality, and personal growth. They work in cooperative teams, endorse collegial efforts, and seek opportunities to work with parents and the community at large. These teachers recognize the importance of sharing experiences and ideas.

As teachers expand their realm of interactions, they recognize how cultural identity plays an important part in the way others react to the world, how they learn, and how they view themselves. Community members and events can be powerful teachers of teachers. Effective teachers learn how to successfully use churches, civic, and community-based organizations as resources and as ways of motivating and encouraging positive growth in students. Exposure to these influences can assist teachers in understanding the frame of reference within which the community's children operate. Connecting the school and community requires that the teacher integrate multicultural education throughout the curriculum. Teachers must be receptive to moving beyond the walls of the school and opening the door to discover the students' other learning environments. The following scenario illustrates how Lee, a secondary mathematics education major, enhanced her student-teaching experiences and promoted the well-being of her students through collaboration and partnerships with colleagues, parents, and the larger community.

### Teaching Scenario

Lee, a math major in secondary education, has completed her student teaching in the Springfield City School District. She enjoyed the diversity she experienced among her assignments in the tenth- to twelfth-grade classrooms at Springfield High School. In addition to her teaching assignments, Lee became involved in an important school/community project.

During her first month at the school, she joined the afterschool tutoring team, sponsored by the Parent Teacher Organization (PTO). This program prepares parents and older adults to tutor students. When she was not busy training tutors, Lee would often work with small groups of students. On several occasions, Lee was assigned responsibility for contacting new parent volunteers and orienting them to the guidelines and curriculum of the program. Her work with the PTO led Lee to several community agencies. One of the PTO members introduced her to the coordinator of the Springfield Parent Partnership Organization, an alternative education program for single parents. Lee was able to interview several parents, recruiting them for the tutoring program. She also visited and interviewed the staff at the Children's Hospital Family Crisis Center and at the Springfield Drug and Alcohol Rehabilitation Center. These experiences helped Lee better understand the needs of some of her students as well as the dynamics of the community in which they live.

Lee gathers artifacts documenting these experiences for Standard Ten in her portfolio. She wishes to demonstrate how she endeavored to foster relationships with school colleagues, parents, and agencies in the larger community and to support students' learning and well-being.

## SAMPLE RATIONALE PAGE

*Artifact for Standard Ten: Partnerships*

*Name of Artifact:* Collection of Documents from Work with
    PTO Afterschool Tutoring Program
*Date:* December 12, XXXX
*Course:* EDE 461—Student Teaching
*Rationale:*
    While student teaching at Springfield High School, I became involved in the Afterschool Tutoring program, sponsored by the PTO. To document my work, I have included my "Volunteer's Log and Journal," which chronicles the experiences I had with the students as well as with the parent volunteers. Also included are samples of student work and a packet of materials I created to use in training parent volunteers for tutoring services.

    My visits to the Springfield Parent Partnership program, the Children's Hospital Family Crisis Center, and the Springfield Drug and Alcohol Rehabilitation Center are documented with letters of inquiry and thank-you notes. The purpose of these visits was to enhance our tutoring program by reaching out to potential volunteers as well as to students in need.

    Finally, I have included a certificate of appreciation from the Springfield PTO. All of these documents portray my ability to coordinate the efforts of parents and community members in the interest of helping students who need tutorial aid in high

*(continued)*

*SAMPLE RATIONALE PAGE (continued)*

school. I believe that programs of this type are most successful when there is a thorough understanding of the impact the community has on its children and when there
is a partnership between the school and its neighboring agencies. My work with the
PTO and its Afterschool Tutoring program reflects my commitment to this belief. The
relationships that I cultivated as a result of this experience will benefit me in the future.
I have learned that partnerships are essential for success in the classroom. I feel confident that I will be able to work with volunteer parent tutors in my future classroom.

## TRY THIS

### Balancing a Portfolio around Teaching Standards

This is a helpful technique for initially organizing a collection of artifacts that you
are considering entering into your professional portfolio and then making meaningful additions to that collection. The goal of this process is achieving a balanced
portfolio where all standards are well documented and a wide variety of types of
artifacts are used.

1. Label a set of expandable file folders, one folder for each of the standards
   you are using. For example, if you are using the INTASC standards, you
   would have ten labeled folders.

2. Attach a sticky note to each artifact in your current collection. On the note
   list all the competencies, skills, and understandings you gained through the
   experience represented by this artifact. Circle the most important of these
   benefits. Find the standard that is most representative of this most important competency. Drop this artifact in the file folder for that standard.

3. When all your artifacts are filed in this manner, use the Artifact Checklist
   found in Appendix B to pencil in which types of artifacts you have chosen
   and under which standards they are filed.

4. When completed, review the checklist of artifacts for balance. Standards
   that are not well documented will become evident. Likewise, you will easily see from this checklist if you have overused certain types of artifacts
   (such as lesson plans) while ignoring other types of artifacts.

5. Make a plan for achieving a more balanced portfolio. You might decide to
   omit some documents that you initially intended to use because they are
   redundant. Then set goals for yourself that will enable you to better document underrepresented standards using a wide variety of types of artifacts.

These goals will enable you to chart the course of your own professional development. Let your goals guide you as you choose meetings and workshops to attend, select journals to read, consider organizations to join, exercise assignment choices wisely, and volunteer for school and community events.

6. Discuss your current checklist of artifacts and your plans for your own professional development with a mentor or instructor. You will no doubt find the insights and suggestions of another professional educator to be invaluable.

# Using the Portfolio throughout a Teaching Career

## The Full Potential of Portfolios

A portfolio is a "proving tool." It provides a body of evidence regarding your professional competencies; in addition, it enables you to be self-aware and self-reflective as you teach. A well-developed portfolio can offer one unique picture of what successful teaching looks like. However, an effective portfolio is not about putting on a good face to appear more competent that you actually are in order to sell yourself to others. To be powerful, a portfolio must be a truthful self-portrait that gives others an accurate picture of where you are in the lifelong journey of professional development. Because it is truthful, it gains the ability to be an "improving tool" as well as a "proving tool." At its best, a portfolio charts an important developmental process in which goals are continually reached and new goals for improvement are set. Portfolio work should raise as many questions as it answers about effective teaching.

Throughout your entire teaching career you will want to know how well you are doing and be able to show others where you are as a professional. For this reason, portfolio work should last the duration of your career. However, your professional portfolio will evolve as your career evolves. Its purposes change; the artifacts chosen for inclusion will change; perhaps your organizational system will change in time. The purpose of this chapter is to show how you can best use a portfolio throughout your career: while studying in a teacher preparation program, while searching for a teaching job, and while serving in a teaching position.

# Using the Portfolio While in a Teacher Education Program

Creating a professional portfolio requires a great deal of time and hard work. However, in this chapter you will be introduced to several motivating reasons for you to commit time, energy, and thought to developing a portfolio. In a portfolio you will have a high-impact, authentic product by which your professional competence can be understood by yourself and judged by others.

## Using a Portfolio to Understand the Profession

As you build a record of your professional growth in a portfolio, you will also gain a vision of the big picture of the world of teaching. You are well advised to build your portfolio around widely accepted standards for the profession. Standards will help you have the end in mind as you study to be a teacher. By focusing on standards you will gain a vision of the destination toward which you're traveling. As you document these standards, you will better understand the roles and responsibilities of a teacher. Your documents will show what competent practice of these standards might look like in actual behavior. Furthermore, as you organize selected artifacts around these standards, you will begin to discern a pattern of how various course assignments and out-of-class experiences fit into this big picture and contribute to your professional development.

## Using a Portfolio to Gain Self-Understanding

You will find as you engage in portfolio development that you will gain a clear picture of yourself as an emerging professional. Your portfolio will provide a record of quantitative and qualitative growth over time in your selected goal areas or standards. A portfolio allows you to see a profile of your strengths and weaknesses. As you connect your work to standards, you can see the value and relevance of your work. A portfolio enables you to reflect on the significance of everyday assignments and experiences with students. You will recognize the value of many out-of-class experiences, such as volunteer work, and you can generate documents to reflect these. In time, you gain an understanding of where you are now and where you are headed. Your portfolio will give you insights into your philosophy and value system as you reflect on what you have determined worth documenting. When you take seriously the value of written reflections on your documents, your portfolio can serve as a scaffold for clarifying your personal teaching philosophy. A portfolio provides a trail of evidence of your progress that will give you a sense of accomplishment and pride. As you gain self-awareness and self-confidence in your professional abilities, you can grow in assuming responsibility for your own continuous professional development. A portfolio can keep in focus what is important to you. Then you can clearly define what you want to accomplish and can take the initiative to achieve this.

## Using a Portfolio to Design Your Own Professional Growth

As you gain more self-understanding, you will become empowered to assume more control over your future learning. You can become a proactive negotiator of your professional development because you have a clear vision of your destination and your goals. To the extent that you have gained an understanding of the profession and of yourself within the profession, you will be equipped to collaborate with professors in individualizing assignments or with advisors in planning a course of study. You and your cooperating teachers in student teaching or early field experiences have a tool in the portfolio for determining the most appropriate teaching experiences for you. As you can see, when you reflect on the portrait your portfolio provides, you will be well positioned to set realistic and meaningful goals for yourself. Autonomous adult learners with an understanding of their profession and of themselves are proactive in all choices and decisions to be made in their education. They enter every learning experience with clear goals in mind. Other ways to become proactive include inviting a professional to be your mentor, developing a peer support group for portfolio work, searching for field placements to best meet your needs, suggesting possible research topics to professors, initiating your own volunteer experiences, and developing a personal professional reading agenda.

## Using the Portfolio to Gain Holistic, Authentic Assessment

Unlike many other forms of assessment, portfolios can capture the complexities of teaching. They have the unique power to make your learning visible. Some teacher preparation programs have portfolio assessment systems in place. In such programs, portfolios will provide faculty members with evidence of their effectiveness in preparing students to meet selected standards. Even if your teacher education program doesn't require portfolios, you should be proactive in presenting your portfolio to others who are assessing your development. For example, you might share your portfolio at an interview where others are determining your readiness for student teaching. It is also advisable to share your portfolio with supervising teachers at field sites and student teaching sites. When you present a portfolio, you are enabling others to assess you broadly, completely, and fairly.

None of the ways to use your portfolio while in a teacher education program will be possible, however, if you delay your portfolio work until the end of your program. When portfolio work is ongoing throughout the entirety of your teacher education program, your portfolio becomes a powerful tool for enabling you to understand your profession, to understand yourself, to become a proactive architect of your own professional development, and to obtain fair and comprehensive assessment of your competence. At the end of your teacher education program, you will have a presentation portfolio that can easily be adapted as an interview tool. However, having an interview portfolio does not guarantee having a successful interview. Interviewing with a portfolio requires thoughtful planning.

# Using the Portfolio When Interviewing for a Teaching Position

Imagine for a moment that you have arrived at an interview for your first teaching position. You are on time, professionally dressed, and armed with a well-developed portfolio. Your interviewer invites you to sit down and begins to ask a barrage of questions. Your mind goes blank; you do not know how to respond to most of the questions. After stammering through them as best you can, you realize that no one has asked to look at your portfolio. Before leaving, you ask the interviewer if he would like to see it. "I'm sure it's really interesting. However, I have several other interviews today and can't spend the time browsing through your portfolio right now. Thanks anyway," he says. You leave with confidence shaken, feeling quite sure that you will not be hired for the position.

How can you avoid such a scenario?

It is imperative to prepare. Your professional appearance and your neatly organized portfolio will probably not be enough. You will need to plan ways to effectively handle questions and incorporate the portfolio into your interview responses. This enables you to present yourself as an effective communicator who can offer specific, concrete documentation of your teaching abilities. Most interviewers prefer that you reference the portfolio during the interview, rather than simply offer it to them to peruse. This saves them time; more importantly, it shows them how well you communicate. Some interviewers may ask you to leave your portfolio with them so that they can later examine it on their own. Still others may not be familiar with portfolios and would not be inclined to initiate discussion about yours. Regardless of the situation in which you find yourself, you can utilize your portfolio to your advantage during the interview—if you are properly prepared.

## Before the Interview

To use your portfolio as an interviewing tool, you will need to do these things well before the interview takes place:

1. Streamline the portfolio so that it contains only the most pertinent documents, based on questions that you anticipate.
2. Create a brochure that summarizes your presentation portfolio.
3. Plan a response to each anticipated question that incorporates your portfolio documents.

Using your portfolio as an interviewing tool means that you will need to present it in a concise and thoughtful manner. To do so, it is necessary to think about the types of questions that will likely be asked in your interview. This can help you streamline, or winnow, the portfolio so that it is a compact picture of your professionalism. Then, you will need to be thoroughly knowledgeable about its contents, so that as you answer the interviewer's questions, you can support your responses with documents and access them instantly. All of this can help you accomplish your goal in the interview—getting the job. Let's look now at the three steps to preparing for the interview with the portfolio.

**Streamline the Portfolio.**    Portfolios can be intimidating to interviewers. Imagine walking into an interview carrying a portfolio that looks like the large-print version of the collected works of Shakespeare. Your portfolio probably includes every valued document and artifact generated during your teacher education program. You are understandably proud of it, and you may want the interviewer to see all that you have accomplished. Unfortunately, no one will ever be as impressed with your work as you and no one will be interested in sitting down and examining every single artifact you have included in your portfolio.

The first step, therefore, in preparing for an interview is to reduce the artifacts in your portfolio to a number that will both support your responses to the interview questions and provide adequate documentation of your strengths and accomplishments as a teacher. This can be a difficult and painful process, for it means removing from the portfolio artifacts and documents in which you invested much time and energy. However, keep in mind that the purpose of the interview presentation portfolio is to showcase your professional competence, and it will not serve this purpose if its size and number of documents overwhelm an interviewer.

A good guideline would be to have no more than two documents or artifacts for each standard contained in your portfolio. Were you to use the ten standards presented in this book that would mean your presentation portfolio would contain no more than twenty artifacts. You should be able to select twenty artifacts that provide a complete picture of your professional skills and abilities. These artifacts will have to be selected with care and be tailored to the specific position for which you are interviewing. Thus, an interview for a kindergarten position might call for artifacts different from those appropriate for an interview for a sixth-grade position. Or, when interviewing with an inner-city school district, you might use different documents from those used with a rural district.

We suggest that your final selections reflect the questions you anticipate being asked in the interview, so that you will be able to present solid documentation of your responses. Such hands-on evidence of your abilities will be appreciated by your interviewers and will showcase your strengths in a compelling way. There are two types of questions that you can expect: general and philosophical questions related to best practice and questions of a more personal nature that ask about your uniqueness.

*General and Philosophical Questions.*    Interviewers will want to gain insights into the kind of educator you are; thus, they will ask questions that probe your knowledge of learning and your dispositions toward teaching. What are they looking for? In general, administrators hire candidates who espouse a practical orientation toward schooling. Interpersonal communication and classroom management are extremely important; therefore, it only makes sense to include at least one artifact in your portfolio that speaks to your communication and management skills. Besides looking for these capabilities, interviewers seek candidates who have adopted the idea that effective teaching is a blend of a variety of direct instruction and facilitative approaches conducted within a sensitive and supportive environment. Essentially, your interviewer wants to see that you are competent in all of the roles of teaching reflected in the standards that comprise your portfolio: planning, assessing, instructing, managing, and forming partnerships.

While administrators place great value on what you know about specific instructional strategies such as cooperative learning, problem solving, critical thinking, and educational technologies, they may also want to know what you have to say about philosophical orientations to teaching and learning. However, they are usually not interested in your ability to label pedagogical or philosophical camps, but rather that you can demonstrate how your classroom practices are based on sound theory. Your interviewer will likely be interested in your understanding of teaching as a reflective practice in which you use a variety of instructional strategies within a cohesive philosophy that meets the needs of all students in the classroom.

Because of this emphasis on your capabilities in the classroom, administrators will want to know about your actual experiences there. Your interviewer will most likely place great importance on any information that you offer about student teaching and field work and will rely on your cooperating teachers' evaluations of your work in their classrooms.

*Questions about Your Uniqueness.* Your interviewer will be interested in your teaching ability; however, he or she may be even more interested in the kind of person you are. Questions about your uniqueness will probably be an important part of your interview. You may be asked about your strengths and weaknesses, your likes and dislikes, your personal goals, the things that motivate you, and the way in which you work with others. For some interviewers, these are high priority questions, because they are trying to determine how well you will "fit" on a team or how well you will represent the school district to parents.

You will want to be prepared to show evidence of your unique strengths. In particular, many interviewers will look to the portfolio for evidence of the attributes about you that make you different from the other candidates. They are interested in documents that reflect, among other things: creativity, positive attitude, professionalism, organizational skills, writing ability, technology skills, potential to succeed, goal setting, leadership, effort, achievements, honors, and awards.

Therefore, before the interview takes place, study your portfolio and look for documents in your portfolio that would support your answers to these two types of questions. Commonly asked questions are listed in Figures 5.1 and 5.2.

| Anticipated Questions of a General/ Philosophical Nature | INTASC Standard(s) | Supporting Portfolio Documents |
|---|---|---|
| What is your educational philosophy? | (Varying, depending on your philosophical orientation and how you present it.) | Article summaries or critiques<br>Anecdotal records<br>Essays<br>Letters to parents<br>Philosophy statement |
| What does an ideal classroom look like? | 2, 4, 5, 7 | Bulletin board ideas<br>Essays<br>Floor plans<br>Lesson plans<br>Letters to parents<br>Management and organization strategies<br>Observation reports<br>Pictures and photographs<br>Portfolios (student)<br>Projects (performance-based)<br>Seating arrangement diagrams<br>Teacher-made materials<br>Theme studies<br>Unit plans |
| How would you assess children's work? | 3, 8 | Assessments (formal and informal)<br>Case studies<br>Interviews with students, teachers, parents<br>Lesson plans<br>Portfolios (student)<br>Problem-solving logs<br>Projects (performance-based) |
| How do you work with parents and other members of the community? | 10 | Community resources documents<br>Field trip plans<br>Interviews with students, teachers, parents<br>Letters to parents<br>Problem-solving logs<br>Professional organizations and committees list<br>Projects<br>Volunteer experience descriptions |

**FIGURE 5.1**   Anticipated Questions of a General/Philosophical Nature and Possible Portfolio Documents to Support Your Answers

*(continued)*

| Anticipated Questions of a General/ Philosophical Nature | INTASC Standard(s) | Supporting Portfolio Documents |
|---|---|---|
| How would you handle discipline problems? How would you manage your classroom? What kinds of management strategies do you like to use? | 5 | Classroom management philosophy<br>Cooperative learning strategies<br>Field trip plans<br>Floor plans<br>Journals<br>Letters to parents<br>Management and organization strategies<br>Observation reports<br>Pictures and photographs<br>Problem-solving logs<br>References<br>Rules and procedures descriptions<br>Schedules<br>Seating arrangement diagrams<br>Student contracts |
| Explain what you know about using technology in the classroom. | 6 | Computer programs<br>Media competencies<br>Projects<br>References |
| What kinds of instructional strategies do you use? When? How well do they work? | 4 | Curriculum plans<br>Evaluations<br>Lesson plans<br>Observation reports<br>Peer critiques<br>Pictures and photographs<br>Projects<br>References<br>Teacher-made materials<br>Theme studies<br>Unit plans |
| How do you meet individual needs in the classroom? | 3 | Individualized plans<br>Interviews with students, teachers, parents<br>Journals<br>Lesson plans<br>Portfolios (student)<br>Problem-solving logs<br>References<br>Student contracts |

**FIGURE 5.1** Continued

| Anticipated Questions of a General/ Philosophical Nature | INTASC Standard(s) | Supporting Portfolio Documents |
|---|---|---|
| What textbooks and other resources have you used in the classroom? How do they compare to others? | 1, 4, 7 | Curriculum plans Projects Theme studies Unit plans |

**FIGURE 5.1**    Continued

Corresponding supporting portfolio documents are listed next to each question; the source of these document types is the artifact possibilities list in Chapter 6 of this text. We have listed only the documents that would reflect authentic and practical work with children, teachers, and parents, because these are the documents that administrators are most interested in seeing as part of your portfolio. Keep in mind that because your portfolio is unique, you may have other documents that will support these questions equally as well. Appropriate INTASC standard numbers are listed next to each of the anticipated questions, so that you can refer to those sections in your portfolio for additional documents. Figure 5.1 lists questions of a general and philosophical nature. Figure 5.2 shows anticipated questions that focus on the teacher candidate as a person. Check your portfolio against these two lists. You will see how well it can be used as an interviewing tool.

After you have examined the charts in Figures 5.1 and 5.2, do some investigating. Find out some things about the school district to which you are applying. Because your interviewer will want to know if you are the right person for the particular position that is available in that school district, questions that relate to the specific programs that are in place at the school, questions about the local community, and even questions about textbooks that are used by the school may be asked. Many school districts have websites that offer information such as this. Other sources of information are the school district office, the school secretary, neighbors in the community, school board meetings, PTO or PTA meetings, and even the community newspaper. Visit the school district office before your interview and ask for copies of information sent to new parents in the district, curriculum guides, or newsletters. You can also find out the names of textbooks used in the school and obtain copies of them.

You may have some strong documents that support your answers to these specific questions, depending on your student teaching experiences and university classwork. Did you do any textbook evaluations or comparisons? Did you use any

| Anticipated Questions That Focus on Your Uniqueness | INTASC Standard(s) | Supporting Portfolio Documents |
| --- | --- | --- |
| What are your strengths? What is your greatest weakness? | (Varying, depending on your strengths) | Awards/certificates<br>Evaluations<br>Goal statements<br>Letters to parents<br>Media competencies<br>Peer critiques<br>Problem-solving logs<br>Professional organizations and committees list<br>References<br>Self-assessment instruments<br>Transcripts<br>Volunteer experience descriptions<br>Work experience descriptions |
| How well can you work with other people? | 9, 10 | Community resources documents<br>Evaluations<br>Field trip plans<br>Letters to parents<br>Peer critiques<br>Professional organizations and committees list<br>Projects<br>References<br>Volunteer experience descriptions<br>Work experience descriptions |
| Tell me about yourself. | 6, 9, 10 | Awards/certificates<br>Essays<br>Goal statements<br>Letters to parents<br>Peer critiques<br>Self-assessment instruments<br>Subscriptions<br>Transcripts |
| Do you plan to go back to college for an advanced degree? What do you do to keep yourself up to date? | 9 | Meetings and workshops log<br>Professional development plans<br>Professional organizations and committees list<br>Professional readings list<br>Self-assessment instruments<br>Subscriptions |

**FIGURE 5.2** Anticipated Questions That Focus on Your Uniqueness and Possible Portfolio Documents to Support Your Answers

| Anticipated Questions That Focus on Your Uniqueness | INTASC Standard(s) | Supporting Portfolio Documents |
|---|---|---|
| What work reflected in your portfolio gives you the most pride? | (Varying, depending on your answer) | (A great variety of documents is possible; this depends on your value judgment) |
| What did your supervisors say about your work? | 9, 10 | Awards/certificates<br>Evaluations<br>References<br>Volunteer experience descriptions<br>Work experience descriptions |
| What do people appreciate about you? | 9, 10 | Evaluations<br>Peer critiques<br>References<br>Volunteer experience descriptions<br>Work experience descriptions |
| What are your goals? | 9 | Goal statements<br>Philosophy statement<br>Professional development plans<br>Self-assessment instruments |
| What is your favorite subject or topic to teach? Why? | 1, 6, 9 | Article summaries or critiques<br>Awards/certificates<br>Computer programs<br>Essays<br>Journals<br>Meetings and workshops log<br>Philosophy statement<br>Pictures and photographs<br>Professional readings list<br>Research papers<br>Self-assessment instruments<br>Subscriptions<br>Transcripts |
| What is your greatest career or academic achievement? | 9, 10 | Awards/certificates<br>Evaluations<br>Journals<br>Peer critiques<br>Pictures and photographs<br>References |

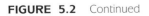

**FIGURE 5.2**   Continued

curriculum guides or teachers' editions of books? Did you work with any assessment tools or tests that are used by this district? Did you complete projects that involved working with children in settings similar to the district? Look back at your work with these materials and reflect upon them. Include documents that will support answers to questions that you anticipate from that particular school district. As another example, suppose you discover that the school district to which you are applying has recently adopted a new hands-on science program. Because of the expense and time put into such a program, it is likely that administrators will be interested in knowing how well you will work with such a program. Thus, you might include a unit plan that you completed during student teaching that shows your use of hands-on strategies for teaching the processes of science. The research that you conduct on the school district to which you are applying should guide you in winnowing your portfolio.

Keep in mind that interviewers are most interested in seeing documents that show authenticity—your capabilities in working well with people and doing real teaching tasks. You may have completed some performance assessments in your education methods classes at the university; these are designed to show your capabilities in the field. Be sure to include documents that show your involvement with teaching, assessing, or observing children, as well as documents that relate to your work with parents and teachers. These documents would be most important, and would take priority over documents such as research papers or essays, which tend to be vicarious rather than experiential.

Once you have found the documents that you can use during your interview to support your answers to possible questions, you need to know exactly where they are located in the portfolio. Remember, administrators are busy people; some of them may even view the portfolio as detrimental to your interview if you are fumbling for documents. Thus, you will need to be able to access documents quickly. Because your portfolio is organized around standards, you have the advantage of having your documents filed under appropriate tabs. Make sure that you know the standard numbers, their corresponding standard categories, and the documents that you have filed there. If you have created an electronic portfolio, you can arrange your home page or compact disk so that each standard is listed, with supporting documents listed directly beneath the standards, much like a table of contents. You or your interviewers can quickly access the document that they wish to see.

Another way to be sure that your portfolio serves you well in the interview is to summarize its most important contents on one page. We suggest the use of a brochure called "Portfolio at a Glance."

**Create a Brochure.**    The "Portfolio at a Glance" (see end of Appendix C) allows you to present your most important artifacts in outline and in a format far more accessible than the complete portfolio. Interviewers might not have the time or the inclination to read the entire contents of a portfolio, but they would find it easy to examine brief descriptions of your significant documents. The brochure is also a potentially far less cumbersome tool to use in an interview situation. Instead of always trying to find a document in a large notebook or on a computer, the artifact can easily be referred to in the brochure. The brochure is something that you can provide every individual participating in the interview and hiring process.

Appendix C provides detailed directions on how to construct a "Portfolio at a Glance." The structure of the brochure is quite simple. You select two artifacts for every standard in your portfolio. Selection of the artifacts used in the brochure should correspond to those you have selected for your interview portfolio. Include in the brochure the names of the documents. Identify the teaching behaviors exemplified in the artifacts. Create a phrase that summarizes and highlights the teaching behaviors you believe each artifact demonstrates. Write two to four statements that describe in more detail the experiences, assignments, and activities undertaken in the creation of the artifact.

The front of the brochure can be personalized in a number of different ways. An email address can be added to your name, address, and phone number. A picture of you in a classroom with children could substitute for the clip art in our example. Anyone examining the brochure would then be able to connect the accomplishments described in the brochure to a name and face. There are other possibilities for the front of the brochure. You might want to quote your mission statement or key concepts from your philosophy. You might want to identify the source of the standards you are using to demonstrate your knowledge of current educational practice. If you have developed a website that includes your professional portfolio, you will want to prominently display its address on the front of your brochure. Also be sure to include a brief set of instructions on accessing your files.

Our sample brochure contains twenty artifacts, two for each of the ten INTASC standards. It does not matter how many standards your portfolio contains, since the format of the brochure is flexible. The advantage and benefit of the brochure lies in its size and accessibility. Multiple copies can be produced and distributed before and during a job interview. The brochure can be attached to a resume and mailed to prospective employers. While computer software makes producing a brochure a little easier, wonderful examples have been created without it.

**Plan Portfolio-Supported Responses to Anticipated Questions.**  Your portfolio is an effective way to present a portrait of your professionalism. When you are asked a question in which the answer is supported in your portfolio, you can take the opportunity to point out this document. We have found that most interviewers prefer that candidates use their portfolio in the interview to add strength to their answers, because doing this presents the candidate as an articulate and well-prepared professional.

Suppose your interviewer asks, "How do you motivate children to learn?" You could simply answer the question, explaining your philosophy of teaching and perhaps describing one of your experiences. But using the portfolio can make your answer come alive and can provide your interviewer with concrete evidence of your capabilities.

To use our example, suppose you taught an exciting lesson during student teaching that utilized the children's interest in a subject. You could say, "One of the most important ways to get children motivated to learn is to interest them. I taught a lesson last semester in which I capitalized on the interests of my fourth graders. I spent a few minutes with them prior to the lesson, brainstorming some topics that would be applicable to my objective, then used these topics as choices for their written reports. This plan, along with some pictures and samples of student work, is in my portfolio."

To successfully use the technique of referencing your portfolio, you need to rehearse your interview. Your posture, your body language, and your verbal responses all need to have a "trial run" prior to your appointment. You should do this by rehearsing alone and by rehearsing with a trusted friend or colleague.

First, rehearse alone. One of the best ways to do this is to use visual imagery. Close your eyes and picture yourself smartly dressed and confident. Imagine yourself arriving at the interview site a few minutes early. Now, in your mind's eye, picture yourself in all the things you do and say from the moment you walk in the door. Put yourself in the best possible scenario, in which you are in control of your answers. Picture your interviewer, who is pleased with your answers and impressed with your portfolio. This positive visual imagery is an important step in building your confidence.

Next, rehearse with a trusted friend or colleague. Give him or her a list of questions that you anticipate. Practice answering those questions, using portfolio documents to support two or three answers. Remember to use Standard English as you talk, look at your interviewer in the eye, and straighten your posture. Ask for honest and constructive feedback. It may be helpful for your mock interviewer to write down some suggestions. Figure 5.3 shows a feedback form that facilitates this.

## The Interview

Once you have secured an interview, there are several things that you can do to make it as successful as possible:

1. Make your portfolio available for previewing.
2. Pay attention to the impression you give to everyone you meet.
3. Introduce your portfolio.
4. Listen for probes and use them as opportunities to provide documentation to your answers.
5. Emphasize your practical experiences.
6. Make all of your responses positive ones.

**Make Your Portfolio Available for Previewing.**    Some administrators who frequently conduct interviews highly recommend that you make the portfolio avail-

---

*Peer Feedback Form: Mock Teacher Interview*

1. What does my nonverbal communication portray?
   (Do I look confident? Nervous? Attentive?)

   What suggestions can you make for improving my nonverbal communication?

2. What is my voice quality?
   (Do I sound confident? Nervous? Enthusiastic?)

   What suggestions can you make for improving my voice?

3. How well do I use my portfolio in the interview?
   (Is my use of documents smooth and quick? Do I appear to know the contents of the portfolio well?)

4. What suggestions can you make for improving my use of the portfolio in the interview?

---

**FIGURE 5.3**    Peer Feedback Form for Making Suggestions after a Mock Interview

able to them prior to your interview. Many interviewers make it a practice to review the candidate's resume a day or two before an interview. If a portfolio were available at that time, this too could be reviewed at the leisure of the interviewer.

One of the advantages of creating an electronic portfolio is that it makes this step of the process very simple; you can simply leave with the administrator a labeled disk or CD on which you have saved your portfolio. Be sure to also include a short letter that introduces yourself. In this letter, be specific. Address it to the person in charge of the interview and specify the teaching position for which you are applying. Also make sure to include brief, clear instructions for accessing your electronic portfolio.

If your portfolio consists of hard copies in a notebook, decide if you are comfortable leaving it with others. If you are, we recommend that you make available your brochure, your portfolio, and an introductory letter about three days before the interview.

If you have both types of portfolios—a notebook of hard copies and its electronic equivalent—leave the disk or CD with your interviewers so that they can access it prior to the interview. Leave also an introductory letter, in which you give instructions for accessing the electronic file. In the letter, also tell them that you have a notebook of hard copies that you will bring with you to the interview.

**Pay Attention to Your Demeanor.**   Even before the interview begins, judgments may be made about you. Your appearance, your punctuality, how you spent time while waiting for the interview, your handshake, and the way in which you filled out any application forms are all part of the total picture that you present of yourself. It is important to remember that your interviewer is not the only person making these judgments: Secretaries, receptionists, and faculty members who meet you as you enter their offices will also take notice of your demeanor.

It is extremely important to be punctual; therefore, it is advantageous to make sure that you arrive just a bit early. Ten to fifteen minutes of "cushion" time enable you to circumvent any unforeseen situations that might occur, such as traffic jams, making a wrong turn, or spilling coffee on your suit. Be careful not to arrive too early, though, as this can interrupt the business of the office.

Once you have arrived, use this time wisely. If you must wait for your interview, seize the opportunity to learn more about the school district. Often lobby areas have newsletters, yearbooks, bulletins, or other such printed material on display and available to the public. These publications can offer valuable information about the school in which you would like to teach, and reading them while you are waiting is just one subtle way of showing your potential employer that you are truly interested in this position.

If you are asked to fill out any application forms or paperwork, pay attention to your handwriting. After all, this is a teaching position that you seek; neatness and letter formation are important, especially in the elementary grades. Someone will notice if your writing is illegible or sloppy.

Be alert. Seat yourself so that you can see and hear as much as possible. You will want to be ready when your name is called and you are invited into the interviewing room. Offer your hand for a handshake and make it firm.

**Introduce Your Portfolio.**   Interviewers indicate that it is not uncommon for an applicant to bring a portfolio into an interview and then never refer to it. Other applicants mention the portfolio only at the end of the interview when time is short. It is a mistake to assume that an interviewer will initiate questions or comments about your portfolio. Also, be aware that time allocations are usually fixed. For these reasons, it is important at the beginning of the interview to indicate that you are prepared with a professional portfolio. There are always a few moments of introductions and informal conversation at the beginning of an interview. During this time make a simple statement such as, "I have with me today my professional portfolio organized around ten national standards for beginning teachers. Here is a brochure outlining the contents of my portfolio. I would be happy to share with you anything from my portfolio that interests you or to circulate my portfolio."

Then follow the interviewer's lead in these matters. A well-done brochure captures your portfolio in a concise and intriguing way and is likely to invite questions about the work reflected in your portfolio. Even if you never have the opportunity to circulate your portfolio, your interviewer will have in hand an effective summary of your competencies in addressing important standards for teachers. The brochure will also be a helpful reference for you to use should you want to quickly locate a particular artifact during the interview. Administrators have told us that they value this type of initiative by the candidate. Introducing your portfolio and presenting a brochure that summarizes your portfolio show that you are organized, politely assertive, capable of summarizing a lot of information, and truly interested in getting this job.

**Listen for Probes.**   Often the interviewer will ask a question, and upon receiving your answer, will ask you to pursue your answer further. This is a probe and an opportunity to use your portfolio to your advantage. For example, suppose the interviewer asks, "How well can you work with others?" You answer by saying, "I am a real team player. I enjoy group work because it gives me the chance to combine my talents with those of other people to get things done." Then, your interviewer probes, "Well, what kinds of groups have you worked with? Tell me more about them." This is where your portfolio will be very handy. You can say, "In my portfolio, filed under 'Standard Ten, Partnerships,' I have included a project that I completed while in college. It is a thematic unit book that three of my colleagues and I worked on together for an entire semester. It is quite a collaborative effort, because the entire team was responsible for making it a success. As you can see, it contains lots of valuable resources for teaching a unit on the environment. In fact, my supervising teacher asked to borrow it for a unit she did with her fifth graders and was very excited about it. She even mentioned it in her reference letter, which is also filed under 'Standard Ten.'"

Such probes invite you to support your answers with additional information, which is the purpose of bringing your portfolio to the interview. Listen carefully for these opportunities and point out any supporting documents that you can. It is not necessary to physically locate each artifact that you mention; in fact, you will want to let the interviewer decide whether to look at these documents. What's most important is that you tell him or her that the information is there and available for careful scrutiny if needed.

**Emphasize Your Practical Experiences.**   All of the work that you have showcased in your portfolio is important. However, your interviewers will be most interested in your work that is authentic and reflective of the kinds of things that teachers do on a daily basis. Thus, whenever you can, back up your answers with documentation from field work and student teaching. When appropriate, point out the reference letters that you have received from cooperating teachers, as well as any performance-based documents you have.

If you answer a question philosophically, be sure to follow up by showing the interviewer your actual experiences. For example, suppose you are asked, "What is your philosophy of teaching?" To emphasize your practical experiences, you could say, "I believe that children learn best when they are actively engaged. My teaching style reflects this. This document, filed under Standard Four, 'Multiple Instructional Strategies,' shows how I used a variety of strategies in a simulated experience that I did with third graders in my field class. We simulated events that took place on Ellis Island in the early 1900s, then the students were required to write reports about topics related to immigration. Strategies used include brainstorming, predicting, building background knowledge, and role-playing. I felt that it was important to get the students involved in the subject before having them write, so I chose to use these simulations, rather than simply assign reports and have the students research information. There are some pictures of the simulated experiences and the bulletin board we created, as well as samples of their reports. This is just one example of how my philosophy of teaching emerges when I teach."

**Make All of Your Responses Positive Ones.**    Answer the questions honestly, but answer in positive tones. No one likes to be asked, "What is your greatest weakness?" However, this is a very popular interview question. You will need to be prepared to answer it positively. One way to do this is to turn your weaknesses into goals to be met. For example, if managing classroom behavior was not one of your strengths during student teaching, you could say, "One of my biggest challenges during student teaching was maintaining classroom discipline. I have begun reading some literature on this and my goal for this year is to prevent discipline problems before they begin." You may even want to show your interviewer a document in your portfolio that lists your goals for improving your work in the classroom. In this way, you can show your interviewers that you view "weaknesses" as opportunities to learn and grow.

## After the Interview

Going to an interview is like running a marathon; the best part is when it's over. But your sense of relief and satisfaction will be enhanced if you plan to do a few things. First, you need to make a decision about leaving your portfolio with your interviewer. Then, regardless of what you do with the portfolio, you need to be sure to leave your "Portfolio at a Glance" brochure. Finally, after you leave, you need to write a follow-up letter. Let's take a look at each of these.

**Make a Decision about Leaving Your Portfolio.**    Sometimes interviewers wish to spend more time with the portfolio and may ask you to leave it with them. If you have an electronic portfolio, your decision is easy. Simply leave a disk or CD, a brochure, and some written instructions for accessing the portfolio. If your portfolio is not electronic, you will need to give this issue some thought prior to the interview. Again, decide what you feel comfortable doing. If you do not wish to part with your portfolio, you might suggest that you could bring it back at another time or offer to leave it and pick it up later the same day. Another suggestion is to simply say, "I will need to keep my portfolio but I can leave copies of my brochure, which summarizes its contents." You may also offer to send copies of any documents in the portfolio that intrigue the interviewer.

If you do decide that you are willing to leave the notebook with the interviewer, be sure to make copies of all documents before you go to the interview, so that you can duplicate the portfolio if necessary.

**Leave a Brochure.**   By all means, leave your "Portfolio at a Glance" brochure when the interview is over. The brochure, because it highlights your capabilities and shows how you have documented the standards that govern your teacher education program, is a strong advocate for you in your absence. We suggest leaving a folder or a bound booklet that contains the brochure as well as any other important documents that highlight your achievements and capabilities, such as your resume, copies of transcripts, and letters of reference. Many school districts require you to submit credentials such as the transcript prior to the interview. Thus, these documents may already be available for your interviewers. However, you may want to ask if there are any other documents that would interest the interviewers and offer to send them right away.

**Write a Follow-up Letter.**   All of the authors of this book are parents; thus, we can't resist the opportunity to tell you, "Be sure to say 'thank you.'" As any parent would tell you, writing a letter of thanks is simply the courteous thing to do. After all, in many school districts, competition for teaching positions is fierce, and your interviewers spend lots of time and energy preparing for and conducting interviews. Thank them for the opportunity to talk with them.

A follow-up letter will certainly enhance the impression you have made on your interviewers. It also gives you one more chance to remain in contact with them. In your letter, after saying thanks, you can summarize the highlights of your interview, making sure to mention a document or two in your portfolio. This would help the interviewer remember you, as well as showcase your communication skills.

You should be proud of this milestone you have reached. Graduation from college says many things about you—among them, your perseverance, your academic strengths, and your professional capabilities. With this achievement, you face yet another test—that of getting the job you want. Because you have a portfolio that is organized around teaching standards, you are already well prepared. Using the steps shown in this chapter, you can customize that portfolio to reflect the position you seek and utilize it as a powerful tool during the interview. This, along with some thoughtful self-reflection, will make your interview a positive and empowering experience.

# Using the Portfolio during Inservice Teaching

Once you are hired and begin your professional career as a teacher, you will continue to find the portfolio useful in many ways. The professional portfolio is changing the way teaching is being conducted and assessed. Through the use of evidenced-based documents and factual profiles, teachers are now able to offer authentic and holistic evidence of their teaching effectiveness. The professional portfolio chronicles a teacher's professional development and showcases his or her pedagogy. It is a catalyst for refining one's teaching philosophy and goals and for improving teaching practices.

The professional portfolio will assist you throughout your teaching career. First-year teachers, their assigned mentors, and administrators use portfolios to assist in the induction process. Beginning and veteran teachers have found portfolios useful in defining and managing professional development, improving instruction, evaluating performance, conducting action research, and demonstrating attainment of local, state, and national goals and standards. Master teachers who are candidates for the National Board for Professional Teaching Standards' (NBPTS) prestigious national teaching certificate use portfolios to document accomplishments of the Board's standards in their respective fields.

In this section, we will examine how the professional portfolio can provide you with a multidimensional representation of yourself as a professional and individual. You will discover its value in communicating to others the special talents you bring to the classroom.

## Getting Started: Mentoring and Induction

When you are hired, you will likely be assigned a master teacher as a mentor who will assist you in defining your role and responsibilities as a teacher. Working with a mentor to develop your professional portfolio not only supports the collaborative nature of teaching and learning, but it can also be a fulfilling and transforming experience.

If you developed a presentation portfolio during your preservice experience or for interviewing, you will want to spend time sharing it with your mentor. This will provide the mentor with background regarding your abilities and interests. Your mentor may ask what goals you would like to address as a beginning teacher. These may include goals you identified when you exited the student teaching program or those established as a substitute teacher. Perhaps your goals may be more immediate, such as learning the programs and routines of the school. Discussion around these topics will help you and your mentor establish a support program that is most beneficial to you.

You and your mentor must now determine how to organize your professional portfolio at the inservice stage. (If you did not develop a professional portfolio during your work at the university for preservice training, you will need to refer to

Chapter 2 of this book for guidelines in creating a portfolio.) The premise of this book is that your portfolio is most effective if it is organized around a set of teaching standards or goals; thus, it is necessary to determine which standards you wish to document. Identify the professional standards that best represent your teaching level (primary, intermediate, middle, or high school), content area, or professional role. These might be different from the standards you used as a preservice teacher, and you may want to include goals set by the school and district. The standards you select will be the focal point of your documentation, so be sure that you reach agreement with your administrators about your choice of standards and the kind of evidence that you will include in your portfolio. Agreement on such important issues at the beginning of the year will ensure that your portfolio will be valued as an effective vehicle for your evaluation and advancement in the profession.

The critical perspective offered by the mentor will help you balance your own subjectivity about your teaching when compared to the goals and standards. The portfolio will continue to provide substance and focus throughout the year as you and your mentor define and redefine your strengths and areas in which you need additional support. Each of you will reflect upon experiences in and outside of the classroom in an attempt to explore which curricular and extracurricular activities are best suited for you.

Your mentor can help determine ways to incorporate your experiences in the portfolio. The process of initiating your inservice portfolio produces evidence of your abilities as a beginning teacher. As you progress through your first year of teaching, you will try different techniques and strategies. This process will provide a basis for reflection. Portfolio documents such as assignments, handouts, and student assessments help you to reflect upon the purposes you have for your lessons and the effectiveness of the daily classroom work.

Throughout the first year, the principal and other administrators will be observing you in your new role and conferencing regarding your performance. Your principal will be interested in documentation that supports what you have accomplished and how you have contributed to the school and students. The portfolio will enable you to offer a visual depiction of your achievements through documented episodes of teaching and service to the school. It will also help you and the administrator establish an action plan for improvement and future endeavors.

By the end of the first year, you will have become more confident in your role and responsibilities as a teacher. You will have established the foundation for developing your portfolio and will be ready to begin to explore other ways to use your portfolio throughout your teaching career.

## Use of the Portfolio throughout the Teaching Career

You are now ready to explore new opportunities and avenues of learning within the school and community. Throughout your career you can use the portfolio to assist you in taking charge of professional development opportunities and controlling the direction of your professional growth. Your portfolio, which is organized around a set of standards that you have chosen to document, will help you engage in the processes of self-reflection and self-assessment. This will guide you as you create personal goals, enhance your teaching skills, engage in action research, and make plans for your professional advancement.

**Reflection and Teacher Research.**    Teachers are active producers of knowledge about what works in the classroom and school. Their reflections can prompt critical questions and action research. Contributions by teacher researchers have advanced our understanding of how theory translates into practice and in turn how practice informs theory.

As a reflective practitioner, you will seek creative ways to improve your practice. The portfolio offers a useful framework as you begin to monitor, record, analyze, and document situations that prompt inquiry. The standards that you have chosen to document are guidelines for this inquiry; you can begin to answer your own questions about each of the teaching behaviors and skills that you use on a daily basis in the classroom. This process, known as action research, is one that supports improvement in instruction, and facilitates collaboration with other professionals. Strategies for conducting action research include collecting data, designing and implementing plans, charting progress, collecting additional data, and analyzing results.

At times, you may find yourself involved with a partner or group of teachers working to resolve an issue or desiring to know more about yourselves as professionals. This research may begin as you and your colleagues dialogue about artifacts in your portfolios or share reflections about particular teaching and learning experiences. You and your partner or group may begin to observe other colleagues to further clarify an issue. Together you will isolate the problem and seek out strategies or solutions. Once again, the portfolio offers a framework for collecting and reflecting on the data. In this situation, you will share portfolio work as you search for examples of successful strategies and techniques that may be tested. Once the research is completed, the results are documented in the portfolio.

You may also consider sharing results of your research with other educators through professional journals and presentations at conferences or teacher workshops. These professional activities and the research artifacts generated through them can be included in your portfolio as demonstration of your skills as a teacher researcher. Some common artifacts associated with action research include classroom notes, literature reviews, hypotheses, sample data, rubrics, supporting evidence, and written conclusions.

Teachers who engage in action research eventually become architects of their own professional development. The cycle of action research is continual. As a teacher researcher, you will reflect upon your practice, explore what occurs in your classroom, question the use of specific teaching methods, and test theory; thus, you will begin to lay a foundation for designing your own professional development plan.

**Teachers as Architects of Professional Development.**   Who determines the content, context, and delivery of your professional growth? When you are empowered by your portfolio work, you are the best architect of your own professional development. Yet, as a teacher in the twenty-first century, you will be expected to maintain critical insight into the changing nature of your profession and to utilize strategies that will ensure your students' successes in the future. This challenge requires you to remain abreast of current research and best practices in education. School districts typically offer ongoing education to support the professional development of teachers. In some districts, staff development is delivered to the entire faculty, regardless of specific needs. Other districts use the professional portfolio as an alternative form of professional development.

If your school district encourages you to design your own professional development plan, your portfolio is the perfect tool for doing this. There are several ways to accomplish the goal of inservice professional growth with the portfolio. One way is to use the post-observation conference. During this conference, you and your principal can determine a plan for professional growth based on the standards that are documented in your portfolio, the documented experiences that you need to add to it, and the results of your teaching evaluation. Another way to plan your inservice needs is to develop a professional development proposal based on the outcome of the action research that you have accomplished in your classroom.

Even if you do not have the flexibility to plan your own program, you can use your portfolio to aid in your professional growth. If your school district requires the entire faculty to attend all staff development programs regardless of individual needs, your portfolio is of great value to you in getting the most out of your training. Before attending an inservice training program, examine the documents under each of the standards in your portfolio and determine your needs. Ask yourself the following questions:

1. How does the training program reflect the standards in my portfolio?
2. Are there any standards in my portfolio that I have not yet documented?
3. Are there documents that indicate areas in which I need to improve?
4. What questions do I need to have answered during the training program, so that I can document growth in these areas?
5. What kinds of experiences or strategies can I add to my teaching repertoire as a result of the training program? How do these experiences or strategies add to my professional growth and how can I document them in my portfolio?

Regardless of the type of program in which you participate, you will want to continually update your portfolio to reflect your new skills and expertise. This will assist you in providing documentation for tenure, advancement, and continued employment.

## Teacher Evaluation and Advancement

Portfolios are being recognized as tools for supporting teacher evaluation, rewarding outstanding practice, issuing permanent certification and license, awarding advancements, and certifying accomplished practitioners. Some of the benefits from using your portfolio to support these endeavors are listed below.

1. Portfolios provide a complete and valid account of what you know and can do.
2. Portfolios supply baseline documentation for ongoing assessment and teaching evaluations.
3. Portfolios offer an authentic view of learning and teaching over time.
4. Portfolios provide principals and other administrators documentation that supports traditional evaluation forms and checklists.
5. Portfolios paint a holistic picture of the candidate seeking promotion and advancement.

Administrators who recognize the value of using portfolios for expanding the evaluation system have transformed their roles from critic or judge to that of coach and education partner. As they examine portfolios, they look for the complexities of teaching and consider the multiple assessments available. Your role is to interpret the various portable documents that support your evaluation. During a conference following an observation of your teaching or during a periodic review, you may find that the administrator will invite you to share your assessment of the performance and cite evidence to support your conclusions. He or she may ask you questions such as:

1. How can this teaching experience contribute to your professional portfolio?
2. What professional goals have you achieved?
3. What successes have you encountered in the development of your portfolio?
4. Where are you experiencing difficulty and how may I assist?
5. How have you contributed to school and district initiatives?

Following each evaluation, you and the administrator should reflect upon the evaluation experience and establish new goals for professional growth. You should update your portfolio to reflect this recent evaluation and include new goals.

Some of the common artifacts used to support evaluations include peer reviews, student evaluations, awards, curriculum and educational resources, grants, and descriptions of contributions you have made to the school and community.

In addition to teacher performance, the portfolio has also contributed to evaluation for the purposes of preservice certification testing; approving candidates for initial certification; awarding master level certification; granting promotions, licensing, and certifications; and supporting program and curriculum evaluation. One of the most noted organizations currently using the portfolio to determine the award of certification is the National Board for Professional Teaching Standards (NBPTS).

## The Master Teacher and the Portfolio

In 1987, the NBPTS was organized to establish a voluntary advanced certification system for the nation's experienced and accomplished teachers. The Board proposed standards representing the knowledge and skills accomplished teachers should possess based upon a two-part assessment system. The first part of the assessment requires that teachers assemble a portfolio of their practice. The second part requires the candidates to spend time at an assessment center where they complete a series of written exercises that probe the depth of their subject-matter knowledge as well as their understanding of how to teach those subjects to their students.

The portfolio, referred to as the school-site portfolio, is scored as part of the assessment. Candidates are instructed to construct portfolios over a selected time period (approximately five months). As a candidate for National Board certification, you would be required to demonstrate evidence of good teaching practices and document how your teaching meets the certification standards, similar to the documentation of standards that we recommend in this book. The list below shows some of the types of activities that you would need to undertake for the NBPTS.

1. Create and critique videos that contain key lesson components.
2. Provide detailed commentaries that conceptualize and document the effectiveness of your practice.
3. Analyze and evaluate student responses to your teaching.
4. Provide in-depth written reflections on your teaching practices.

For all documents in your school-site portfolio, you would need to write goals and purposes, rationales supporting your professional judgments, and reflections.

## Your Portfolio and Your Teaching Career

The portfolio as a "proving tool" and an "improving tool" is a valuable part of all phases of your teaching career. While it is a vital component of your interview when becoming a new teacher, it is much, much more than that. Organized around the standards that are important to your profession, it helps you to be an autonomous learner, but it also gives you an opportunity to showcase your strengths to your professors and supervisors during your teacher education program, as well as to your potential employers. Continuing to develop your portfolio as an inservice teacher enables your professional growth and advancement. The portfolio development process gives you a way to reflect upon your own teaching practices, document your action research, support the inservice training that is required of you, prepare for recertification, and begin to experience the process required of National Board Certification. Your professional teaching portfolio helps you know how well you are doing, while it shows others the same. That is its full potential.

## TRY THIS

### 1. Identifying Strengths and Weaknesses

This chapter explains how you can use the professional portfolio as an "improving tool" throughout your career. Part of your professional growth is about identifying your strengths and weaknesses as a teacher. The following exercise shows you how to do this.

1. Think of a teacher you admire and respect. What specific characteristics did this teacher have that made an impact on you? Write a paragraph that answers this question.

2. In your paragraph, highlight the specific characteristics or qualities that positively impacted you as a student.

3. Make a list of these characteristics.

4. Think about how your own personal or professional characteristics and qualities align with the characteristics on this list.

5. Make a list of things related to teaching that you do well, called "My Strengths."

6. Make a list of things related to teaching that you need to improve, called "My Weaknesses."

7. Place these informal lists in the front pocket of your portfolio notebook or in a file in your electronic portfolio. These lists can help you get started with your own professional growth, seek opportunities to meet your challenges, and focus on the strengths that define you as a teacher.

Look at the following example.

### The Teacher I Admire and Respect: Ms. Acaba

I remember that Ms. Acaba was **flexible** with the topics that we learned. While teaching a unit on South America, she realized that a **hands-on experience** would help us learn more about an important industry of the countries in that continent. Thus, she arranged for us to visit a local coffee plant and tour the facility. In addition, even though the study of Spanish was not specifically in our curriculum, as a native Puerto Rican and a fluent Spanish speaker, she used her **expert knowledge of the subject** to encourage us to practice the language in the classroom. She also guided us with **authentic assignments** like a classroom newsletter and a fashion show of traditional South American dress. She created a parent volunteer schedule for adults who were able to help with these activities. I remember her as being **kind, considerate, patient,** and **nonjudgmental.** I was particularly grateful that she **did not show favoritism** in her classroom.

### Ms. Acaba's Teaching Characteristics

- Flexible
- Provided hands-on experiences
- Used her expert knowledge
- Gave authentic assignments
- Kind
- Considerate
- Patient
- Nonjudgmental
- Did not show favoritism

| My Strengths | My Weaknesses |
| --- | --- |
| Patient | Unorganized |
| Kind | Not always flexible |
| Easy to talk to | Need practice and confidence with math skills |
| Generous | |
| Excellent communication skills | |
| Believe students learn by doing hands-on things | |

## 2. Reflecting and Sharing

In the final section of this chapter we discuss how your portfolio can be a valuable tool throughout your professional career. We emphasize that reflection—the process by which teachers assess instruction, think critically about pedagogy, analyze subject matter, and focus on the needs and background of their students—is a critical component of the portfolio. We demonstrate how new teachers can engage in reflection as they build their portfolio based upon INTASC Standards. Teachers will continue this process throughout their professional career and build upon their experiences as master teachers who are candidates for National Board Teacher Certification. In the following exercise you will prepare a reflection on your teaching.

Select a lesson plan you have taught that includes a student assignment. Think critically about your plan, instruction, and assessment and then analyze your practice using the following prompts and questions.

- What worked well?

- What did each student learn from the instruction that preceded the assignment?

- What did each student learn from the assignment?

- How specific were your instructions?

- How did you analyze the students' assignment? What did you learn from each student's response?

- What would you do differently as a result of the students' responses to the assignment?

- Would you give the same assignment again? If you would give the same assignment, would you change the preceding lesson or directions?

- If you would change the assignment, what would you do differently? Explain why you would make these changes.

Now, share your written reflection, the original artifact, and this list of prompts and questions with a colleague or master teacher. Discuss your reflection and share what you learned about your students and your pedagogy as a result of this teaching experience. You can also use this exercise as an entry in your portfolio. What INTASC Standard or NBPTS will you select?

# Artifact Possibilities

## How to Use This Chapter

The types of documents listed on the next few pages are possible artifacts for your portfolio. They are explained here so that you may better facilitate their use. Each definition contains two features: a definition of the document as it relates to classes and other learning opportunities and an explanation of the types of teaching skills that this document may reflect. These suggestions do not include all the possibilities that exist as documents. As you create artifacts that make reference to students or teachers, avoid using names or other identifying information. It is always critical to maintain confidentiality.

## Types of Artifacts

### Action Research

Include examples of action research in which you have inquired about ways to improve classroom instruction, student learning, and your own practices. Your investigation can reflect work that you have done alone or as a member of a team of teachers and perhaps other professionals. You should describe how you sought to generate and sustain improvement in teaching and learning as a result of your investigation. You may also highlight certain aspects of the research. Carefully consider the nature of your inquiry and the standard that you have chosen. For example, you may want to consider describing how you progressed through the process by reflecting upon and assessing your teaching practices as you explored new ideas, implemented strategies, and utilized new resources. Regardless of which standard and aspect of inquiry you choose to highlight, remember to always address the impact of your work on students.

## Anecdotal Records

These are notes that you have taken in classroom observations or during your own teaching. They may pertain to any of the following: the intellectual, social, emotional, or physical development of a student or some students; personal observations about instructional decisions that you have made; or personal observations of teachers at work. The notes reflect your assessment or child observation skills, your ability to make instructional plans, or your knowledge of child development.

## Article Summaries or Critiques

You may have written a summary or evaluation of an article from a professional journal as a class assignment. When including these in your portfolio, choose critiques that address the desired topic very specifically. The title of the article should be reflective of a chosen standard, making an obvious connection. This document is especially helpful if your professor has made positive remarks about your work and these remarks are about the outcome you wish to document.

The article summary or critique may show your ability to analyze any number of teaching skills. For example, suppose you critiqued an article titled "Getting Parents Involved in Their Children's Education." If you discussed your own ideas about parent involvement in your critique, this document may be able to reflect your knowledge of school-home-community cooperation.

## Assessments

Any forms of assessment you have used or developed to measure student performance would be included in this type of document. Examples of assessments are performance tasks, portfolios, teacher-written tests, informal observations or notes, evaluations from lesson plans, formative assessment notes or charts, and summative charts of student developmental levels. You may want to include the actual assessment instrument you have written, with the students' work on it, if applicable (only a few copies are necessary). In addition, you may include notes in a personal journal from observations made during the administration of a standardized test. Your ability to assess student's performance, diagnose progress, and use tests wisely is reflected in this document. In addition, your understanding of child development may be evident.

## Awards and Certificates

Copies of letters, awards, or certificates that verify your outstanding contribution to the field of education fit in this category. These could include honors conferred, memberships in honorary professional organizations, community recognition, and volunteer recognition. Your professional commitment is reflected in these types of documents.

## Bulletin Board Ideas

After creating a bulletin board, make a copy of your design or take a photograph of the board. Make sure all spelling, punctuation, and grammar are Standard English. This document can be used to show your ability to think creatively, use materials in interesting ways, or motivate students.

## Case Studies

A case study is a thorough examination of a student's growth over a period of time. When using this as a document, make sure the student is anonymous. Generally, case studies are quite long; therefore, you may want to include a specific part of the paper for documentation of a standard. Your knowledge of human development as well as your observation skills may be evident in this document.

## Classroom Management Philosophy

This is a written summary of your philosophy of classroom management. Make sure to cite the research and theories that have guided you in the way you influence student behavior and encourage development of self-control. Classroom management skills and knowledge of human development are evident in this document.

## Community Resources Documents

These might include copies of actual correspondence or a description of less formal contact between you and a community resource. Have you solicited a community resource to provide information in completing a course assignment or to teach a lesson in the classroom? Did you invite a guest speaker into your classroom during a field class or student teaching? These types of correspondence show that you are able to foster positive relationships between the community and the school.

## Cooperative Learning Strategies

Have you planned or taught a lesson using a cooperative learning technique? Cooperative learning is a method of teaching in which students work collaboratively in small heterogeneous groups to solve a problem. This type of group work must be obvious in your lesson. You may want to include a copy of the lesson plan and, if the lesson was actually taught, a statement assessing the effectiveness of the cooperative learning technique. This will document your ability to use cooperative learning as a strategy as well as your ability to manage and motivate a class of students.

## Curriculum Plans

These documents are written plans, programs, or both designed to organize curriculum. Your curriculum plans can reflect all experiences you have developed for the child while engaged in the process of schooling. Examples may include lesson plans, units, thematic units, learning centers, extracurricular programs, or school-community ventures. These documents portray your instructional planning skills or your ability to use many and varied instructional strategies.

## Essays

You can use papers from education courses, English composition, or any other class in which you were required to write an essay. Examine the topic you addressed in your paper to be sure its main idea reflects one of the standards you are using.

This type of artifact could document almost any standard. A question you wish to answer or the topic you wish to address should be clearly stated at the beginning of the essay. You may want to highlight this, showing its obvious connection to the standard you wish to document. For example, suppose you wrote an essay in a composition class titled "Why Suzy Can't Do Math: The Influence of Societal Expectations." Because this is an essay on the differences that gender may make in the perception of students in the home, in the neighborhood, and in school, your understanding of social influences on the education of females becomes evident, especially if you offer suggestions that show how you would eliminate gender bias in your own math lessons. This would be a good artifact to document your understanding of the individual needs of learners and your ability to create instructional opportunities for everyone in your class.

## Evaluations

Any on-the-job performance assessment is an especially important type of evaluation to include in a portfolio. Student teaching is one place where this will occur. You might include actual observations done when you taught a lesson, feedback on a written assignment, or some kind of summative assessment (interim or final evaluation). Make sure there is a relationship between the evaluation comments and the standard.

## Field Trip Plans

As a preservice teacher, you may have gone on field trips that would be related to one of the standards you have chosen. Trips such as these may include visits to teacher centers, libraries, museums, innovative classrooms, other universities, youth centers, or rehabilitation centers. You may document this by including copies of programs, personal journals, agenda, letters of invitation, or memos.

Your own notes or observational reports are also helpful. This type of document may provide evidence for a variety of standards. Your professional commitment and responsibility are reflected because of your willingness to seek information outside the college classroom.

If you actually planned a field trip for one of your classes, be sure to document this. Record your lesson plans, your correspondence with the community agents involved, your letter to parents, and any other communication you used. This is strong evidence of your planning skills, knowledge of content, knowledge of human development, and school-home-community cooperation.

## Floor Plans

A floor plan is a sketch of the arrangement of space, equipment, and materials you designed in order to meet the needs of a group of students under your supervision. Your ability to use environments and materials appropriately is most closely related to this document. If you include a statement of how this floor plan enhances your classroom management plan, then it also could document your classroom management skills.

## Goal Statements

Professional goals are based on your needs, interests, philosophy of education, and perception of your role as a teacher. Goal statements assist you in determining where you want to be and provide you with information about how to get there.

Think about the important results you should accomplish in your role as a teacher and record these as goal statements. Remember that any short-term goals you establish should be tied to the longer-term goals you have identified in conjunction with your philosophy of education. Periodically review and evaluate your accomplishments in relation to your goal statements. You may wish to list your accomplishments associated with each goal. You will establish new goals as you refine your philosophy of education, your role as a teacher, and your expectations. It is important to keep your list of goal statements current. These statements might appear at the beginning of your portfolio or as documentation of your professional commitment.

## Individualized Plans

Students with special needs sometimes need tasks to be structured in ways that will allow them to use their strengths and compensate for their specific learning difficulties. Ways in which lesson and unit plans have been adapted for specific students should be documented. Make sure the learning need is defined and clearly addressed. This artifact could document your skills in meeting individual needs, your instructional strategies skills, and your knowledge of human development.

## Interviews with Students, Teachers, Parents, or Caregivers

These include planned conversations with a specific agenda. Include a copy of the questions and answers as well as a summary and analysis of the interview. This interview may be part of a case study for one of your classes. Interviews can yield a variety of information; for example, an interview with a student may give you some indication of his or her language development, thus documenting your understanding of human development.

## Journals

You may have kept journals during field classes or observation assignments. Include them if they address your observations of students as they relate to the desired standard. If necessary, highlight the appropriate sections of the journals. Make sure dates and times are included but not the names of schools or teachers visited.

## Lesson Plans

Copies of your lesson plans should include all components of a workable plan: objectives, materials, introduction, procedures, closing, and evaluation. Sometimes plans may be used for more than one standard. In this case, highlight the specific part of the plan that documents the standard. Your ability to execute instructional planning and to use a variety of instructional strategies will be most obviously documented with lesson plans; however, it is possible that knowledge of content, use of environments and materials, communication skills, and knowledge of human development could be documented here.

## Letters to Parents or Caregivers

Include copies of correspondence that was sent home. This could include permission slips, weekly newsletters, requests for help with homework, notices about parties, notification about field trips, requests for family conferences, student award certificates, or letters that explain upcoming activities. Such correspondence could document your cooperation with the home and community as well as your communication skills. Make sure letters contain correct spelling and Standard English grammar.

## Management and Organization Strategies

After trying a particular management or classroom organization strategy, systematically observe and code the events that occurred. This will enable you to record what is important about your experience. Write a brief summary and explanation of your observation. For example, you may have tried a chart system for classroom jobs, a record-keeping device for holistic scoring of writing, a system of recording anecdotal notes, or a way to expedite peer editing during writing classes. These types of explanations reflect your ability to manage the classroom well.

## Media Competencies

This artifact includes evidence and descriptions of the various forms of media you are able to incorporate in your instruction. This could include teaching resources such as the camcorder and VCR, Infocus, computers and printers, interactive video, laser disks, educational television, digital cameras, DVDs, DVRs, and projection devices.

You will also want to include evidence of your ability to incorporate technology into the classroom. Examples of how you have used email, remote databases, PowerPoint, and distance learning equipment to research and to communicate with students and colleagues regionally, nationally, and internationally should be highlighted. A printout, CD, or floppy disk of your Internet address(es), listing of professional online news group and listserv memberships you hold, and examples of printed texts will provide documentation of your ability to share and retrieve information via Internet.

Media competency reflects your ability to utilize a wide range of communication resources, environments, and materials appropriately. Therefore, you may wish to include a checklist of the various media and other state-of-the-art technology you are able to incorporate into your classroom.

## Meetings and Workshops Log

If you have attended meetings or listened to speakers who discussed a topic related to the standard, include a reaction paper plus a copy of the program. These logs would be a good way to document your professional commitment and responsibility.

## Observation Reports

Systematic, regular noticing and recording of behaviors, events, and interactions in the classroom should be a part of every field experience you have. Include brief descriptions of your observations in a variety of grade levels. Reports could be in paragraph or checklist format. Depending upon the focus of your observations, your reports may reflect your knowledge of a variety of standards.

## Peer Critiques

This encompasses formal and informal assessments of you by your classmates. This could include score reports that are made out by classmates during your class presentations. The standard you document with this artifact depends on the presentation that your peers critique. If it was a lesson demonstration, your planning or instructional strategies skills would be evident. Your use of materials, communication skills, or knowledge of human development might also be evident. Make sure the comments made by your peers reflect the standard you are documenting.

## Philosophy Statement

This is a brief position paper or statement of your philosophy of teaching. Make it clear and concrete. You may want to preface your entire portfolio with this statement. Sometimes it is an assignment in a class, but if not, write one on your own. It should include your underlying beliefs about the teaching strategies and practices that are best for students. Either leave out or explain educational jargon; do not include such terms simply because they sound good. If you include the philosophy statement in more than one section, highlight the part that pertains to the specific standard.

## Pictures and Photographs

Include photographs that show active learning in progress, special projects, field trips, or artistic expressions that cannot be physically included in this notebook because of size. Bulletin boards, puppets, learning centers, and trips to museums are just some of the many ideas and activities you may want to photograph. Depending on the photograph, you could document a variety of standards. If it is of a field trip that you took to a professional meeting or conference, document your professional commitment. If it is of a field trip or other related activity in which you participated with a class of students, you may want to document your use of instructional strategies, depending on your involvement in the planning process.

## Portfolio (Student)

A student portfolio is an organized collection of work that demonstrates the student's achievement and performance over time. Various kinds of evidence might be used, including the student's projects, written work, learning journals, and video demonstrations. A sample student portfolio would document your understanding of varied assessment strategies.

## Position Papers

Include scholarly papers written to present an educational issue, viewpoint, or controversy. Be sure that sources are up to date. Papers such as these could document your professional commitment as well as your knowledge of philosophical and social influences.

## Problem-Solving Logs

As you identify professional problems or challenges, record them. It would be helpful to include a clear statement of the problem, alternative strategies for dealing with the problem, the chosen strategies, and the results of the implementation of each of them. Depending on the problem you solved, document your use of instructional strategies, classroom management skills, or your cooperation with the home and community.

## Professional Development Plans

Include a short paragraph or list explaining your short- and long-term plans for professional development. This could include efforts to improve knowledge or performance in specific areas of teaching, attendance and participation in professional organizations or workshops, and plans for earning additional credits in graduate school. This area should reflect where you are now in terms of your profession and where you plan to be within the next few years. Such statements document your professional commitment and responsibility.

## Professional Organizations and Committees List

List and briefly describe your involvement with an organization, committee, or other group that you feel has had an impact on you professionally or personally. Examples could include participation in campus and community organizations. Be sure to include some sort of evidence of your participation in these groups, such as a membership card, a letter of acceptance, or program from an activity. Such memberships show that you actively seek out opportunities to grow professionally.

## Professional Readings List

Keep a list of professional readings you have done and include your reactions to the issues and concepts discussed. Your professional commitment and responsibility are reflected in professional reading lists.

## Projects

Projects can include any type of assignment that involved problem solving, group presentations, creating materials, investigating phenomena in classrooms, or researching current information. In a presentation portfolio, include paper copies only and make photographs of anything too large to fit in a notebook. If this is a group project, make that clear but indicate the extent of your input. (Be careful about this one; it is not helpful to brag about doing all the work.) The documentation possibilities of this artifact depend on the project. Examine the standards to determine whether the project reflects instructional planning skills, professional commitment, the ability to meet individual needs, or knowledge of content.

## References

References might include statements, evaluations, or both, from your supervisors of your academic work, experiences in the classroom, other work experience with children, or outside employment. Try to connect the reference with one of your selected standards. For instance, the reference might describe a lesson you taught in a field course or in student teaching. You could use this document to illustrate your competence in the area of instructional strategies. In addition, you may want to place reference letters from your cooperating teachers in a special tabbed section of the portfolio.

## Research Papers

When selecting a research paper to include in your portfolio, you will need to consider several factors. The content of the research paper might make it appropriate for inclusion under a particular standard. It might, for instance, highlight your knowledge of an academic subject.

## Rubrics

Include examples of rubrics you have developed or selected to measure student performance. You may also describe how you instructed students to use the rubric as a tool for self-assessment. Be certain your rubric offers a set of categories that define and describe the important components of the work being assessed. This includes gradation of levels of completion or proficiency with a score assigned to each level and a description of what criteria need to be met to attain that score at each level. Since the criteria for assessment are clearly defined, you may choose to share examples of how this enabled you and your students to share a common understanding of the assignment's goals and criteria and the various levels of completing the defined criteria.

## Rules and Procedures Descriptions

While you were student teaching or perhaps during field classes, you may have had the opportunity to write your own classroom rules or procedures. This document should describe the regular, repeated guidelines or routines for behavior that give your classroom predictability and order. These descriptions of rules should give some evidence of your ability to manage the classroom and create an environment conducive to learning and positive interaction.

## Schedules

During student teaching, you were probably asked to complete a daily schedule. If you use this as a document, be sure that it clearly describes your format for the events of the day for students under your supervision. The order of events and the length of time allotted to each should be clear and concise. Classroom management skills are reflected in this type of artifact.

## Seating Arrangement Diagrams

A particular seating arrangement (such as having students sit in groups) might complement a particular teaching strategy (such as cooperative learning). It might also reflect a particular classroom management need, such as seating certain students apart from the rest of the class. Your ability to plan for instruction, use environments, and manage the classroom could be documented with this artifact.

## Self-Assessment Instruments

This includes results from instruments, rating scales, surveys, or questionnaires that provide feedback about your performance. This shows your professional commitment and responsibility. Self-assessment instruments also include examples of instruments you developed to engage students in measuring their own performance (cognitive, affective, and psychomotor). These could document your assessment skills.

## Simulated Experiences

Include an explanation of educational experiences in which you learned through the use of simulation as a teaching method. A simulation is an activity that represents a real-life experience. This activity could include teaching an elementary lesson in a methods class, dramatizing a simulated classroom management scenario, or some other type of role-play experience. Describe the simulation, its purpose, and what you feel you learned from the experience. The simulation itself will determine the standard you can document.

## Student Contracts

You may have the opportunity to write individual (one-on-one) contracts to help promote a student's academic achievement or improved behavior. The actual contract should look formal—it should be typed and specifically spell out the conditions under which the terms of the contract (achievement, behavior, and so on) will be met. In addition, it should include spaces for the teacher and the student to sign, date, and confirm their agreement to the conditions. You may not have the need to draw up contracts until you student teach, but you may see some in use during your field experiences. (Classroom management rules that all students are expected to follow do not qualify under this category.) This type of artifact reflects your ability to develop learning experiences on the basis of diagnosis and observation, or perhaps it can document your classroom management skills, depending on the reason for the individual contract.

## Student Work

The actual work that your students produce is one of the most important indicators of your effectiveness as a teacher. You should include in your portfolio representative samples of student projects and assignments as well as videotapes of student performances. Whenever possible, you should include the criteria or rubric you used to evaluate this work. Your portfolio would not be complete unless it documents how you are attaining student learning results while simultaneously mastering initial teaching competencies. Remember to always remove students' names from their work and obtain parent or guardian permission to photograph or videotape.

## Teacher-Made Materials

These materials may include games, manipulatives, puppets, big books, charts, videotapes, films, photographs, transparencies, teaching aids, costumes, posters, or artwork. Because many of these items are cumbersome, include only paper copies or photographs of the materials. If you do not have copies of the actual materials you have made, you may want to highlight sections of a well-designed lesson plan that show how you would use creative teaching materials. Materials that support learning theory and were designed to suit this purpose are most helpful. Your materials should reflect your ability to encourage active learning and a variety of instructional strategies.

## Technological Resources

Examples of various programs you have utilized, developed, or incorporated in your teaching provide evidence of your ability to use materials in a challenging and appropriate way to encourage active learning.

Also appropriate are documents that demonstrate your ability to conduct online searches and research. Examples include ERIC, Education Index, and Internet programs that link teachers worldwide. You can document your abilities by providing the hard copies of these searches along with an explanation of the reason for your online searches. These documents reflect your willingness to seek further professional growth.

## Theme Studies

This is a set of lesson plans or resource materials that fit a central theme. Theme studies integrate many subjects, which might include math, science, health, physical education, English, social studies, reading, art, music, and spelling. Make sure that your plans contain all elements of good lesson plans and are obviously related to your overall theme. Your knowledge of a variety of instructional strategies should be evident through your use of computer programs, children's literature, manipulatives, films, charts, or concrete materials. In addition, your instructional planning skills will be evident.

## Unit Plans

A unit is an integrated plan for instruction on a topic developed over several days or even weeks. Often, units are developed within a discipline, and lessons are organized to build on knowledge acquired in previous lessons. Unit plans generally include purposes, objectives, content outlines, activities, instructional resources, and evaluation methods. (Interdisciplinary units have been described under the entry called Theme Studies.) Unit plans are particularly good for documenting your ability to use a variety of instructional strategies and instructional planning skills.

## Video Scenario Critiques

Often in university methods courses, professors will ask you to view and critique a videotape of actual teaching scenarios. If you wish to include a critique you have completed, be sure to describe the scenario and give its bibliographical information. Make sure the critique speaks to the standard you plan to document. Depending on the nature of the video, there are several possibilities for documentation.

## Volunteer Experience Descriptions

This document might include a list and brief description of volunteer experiences and services provided to the school and community. You should focus on how these activities have enhanced your teaching abilities while providing a contribution to society. You should also emphasize the importance of maintaining positive school-community collaboration through teacher, parent/caregiver, and student interaction.

## Work Experience Descriptions

These are statements you have written to describe work experiences. These might include work with students in both traditional and nontraditional settings and work for which you were compensated or that you performed on a voluntary basis. To be of most interest, these statements should include not only a summary of the setting and your responsibilities but also a reflective statement addressing the intangible aspects of the work experience. In writing these statements, be sure to address how these work experiences relate to the specific standard.

# NCATE-Affiliated Professional Organizations

Many professional organizations have developed standards for teachers. A good source of standards is the member organizations of the National Council for Accreditation of Teacher Education (NCATE). NCATE is a nonprofit, nongovernmental organization recognized by the U.S. Department of Education as the accrediting body for colleges and universities that prepare teachers and other school personnel. Over 525 institutions are accredited by NCATE.

Most of the 33 professional organizations listed below have standards around which you could organize your portfolio.

### Teacher Education Organizations
American Association of Colleges for Teacher Education (AACTE),
    http://www.aacte.org/
Association of Teacher Educators (ATE), http://www.ate1.org/

### Teacher Organizations
American Federation of Teachers (AFT), http://www.aft.org/
National Education Association (NEA), http://www.nea.org/

### State and Local Policymaker Organizations
Council of Chief State School Officers (CCSSO), http://www.ccsso.org/
National Association of State Boards of Education (NASBE),
    http://www.nasbe.org/
National School Boards Association (NSBA), http://www.nsba.org/

**Specialized Professional Organizations—Subject Specific Organizations**
American Council on the Teaching of Foreign Languages (ACTFL),
    http://www.actfl.org/
American Alliance for Health, Physical Education, Recreation and Dance
    (AAHPERD), http://www.aahperd.org/
International Reading Association (IRA), http://www.reading.org/
International Technology Education Association (ITEA),
    http://www.iteawww.org/
National Council for the Social Studies (NCSS), http://www.ncss.org/
National Council of Teachers of English (NCTE), http://www.ncte.org/
National Council of Teachers of Mathematics (NCTM), http://www.nctm.org/
North American Association for Environmental Education (NAAEE),
    http://www.naaee.org/
Teachers of English to Speakers of Other Languages (TESOL),
    http://www.tesol.org/

**Specialized Professional Organizations—Child-Centered Organizations**
Association for Childhood Education International (ACEI),
    http://www.acei.org
Council for Exceptional Children (CEC), http://www.cec.sped.org/
National Association for the Education of Young Children (NAEYC),
    http://www.naeyc.org/
National Middle School Association (NMSA), http://www.nmsa.org/

**Technology Organizations**
Association for Education Communications and Technology (AECT),
    http://www.aect.org/
International Society for Technology in Education (ISTE), http://www.iste.org/

**Specialist Organizations**
American Educational Research Association (AERA), http://www.aera.net/
American Library Association (ALA), http://www.ala.org/
Council of Learned Societies in Education (CLSE),
    http://www.members.aol.com/caddogap/clsehome/htm
National Association of School Psychologists (NASP),
    http://www.nasponline.org/

**Administrator Organizations**
American Association of School Administrators (AASA), http://www.aasa.org/
Association for Supervision and Curriculum Development (ASCD),
    http://www.ascd.org/
National Association of Black School Educators (NABSE), http://www.nabse.org/
National Association of Elementary School Principals (NAESP),
    http://www.naesp.org/
National Association of Secondary School Principals (NASSP),
    http://www.nassp.org/

**Other**
National Board for Professional Teaching Standards (NBPTS),
    http://www.nbpts.org/

# Artifacts Checklist

|  | 1 | 2 | 3 | 4 | 5 | 6 | 7 | 8 | 9 | 10 |
|---|---|---|---|---|---|---|---|---|---|---|
| Action Research |  |  |  |  |  |  |  |  |  |  |
| Anecdotal Records |  |  |  |  |  |  |  |  |  |  |
| Article Summaries or Critiques |  |  |  |  |  |  |  |  |  |  |
| Assessments |  |  |  |  |  |  |  |  |  |  |
| Awards and Certificates |  |  |  |  |  |  |  |  |  |  |
| Bulletin Board Ideas |  |  |  |  |  |  |  |  |  |  |
| Case Studies |  |  |  |  |  |  |  |  |  |  |
| Classroom Management Philosophy |  |  |  |  |  |  |  |  |  |  |
| Community Resources Documents |  |  |  |  |  |  |  |  |  |  |

*(continued)*

|  | 1 | 2 | 3 | 4 | 5 | 6 | 7 | 8 | 9 | 10 |
|---|---|---|---|---|---|---|---|---|---|---|
| Cooperative Learning Strategies |  |  |  |  |  |  |  |  |  |  |
| Curriculum Plans |  |  |  |  |  |  |  |  |  |  |
| Essays |  |  |  |  |  |  |  |  |  |  |
| Evaluations |  |  |  |  |  |  |  |  |  |  |
| Field Trip Plans |  |  |  |  |  |  |  |  |  |  |
| Floor Plans |  |  |  |  |  |  |  |  |  |  |
| Goal Statements |  |  |  |  |  |  |  |  |  |  |
| Individualized Plans |  |  |  |  |  |  |  |  |  |  |
| Interviews with Students, Teachers, Parents, or Caregivers |  |  |  |  |  |  |  |  |  |  |
| Journals |  |  |  |  |  |  |  |  |  |  |
| Lesson Plans |  |  |  |  |  |  |  |  |  |  |
| Lettters to Parents or Caregivers |  |  |  |  |  |  |  |  |  |  |
| Management and Organization Strategies |  |  |  |  |  |  |  |  |  |  |
| Media Competencies |  |  |  |  |  |  |  |  |  |  |
| Meetings and Workshops Log |  |  |  |  |  |  |  |  |  |  |
| Observation Reports |  |  |  |  |  |  |  |  |  |  |
| Peer Critiques |  |  |  |  |  |  |  |  |  |  |

|  | 1 | 2 | 3 | 4 | 5 | 6 | 7 | 8 | 9 | 10 |
|---|---|---|---|---|---|---|---|---|---|---|
| Philosophy Statement |  |  |  |  |  |  |  |  |  |  |
| Pictures and Photographs |  |  |  |  |  |  |  |  |  |  |
| Portfolio (Student) |  |  |  |  |  |  |  |  |  |  |
| Position Papers |  |  |  |  |  |  |  |  |  |  |
| Problem-Solving Logs |  |  |  |  |  |  |  |  |  |  |
| Professional Development Plans |  |  |  |  |  |  |  |  |  |  |
| Professional Organizations and Committees List |  |  |  |  |  |  |  |  |  |  |
| Professional Readings List |  |  |  |  |  |  |  |  |  |  |
| Projects |  |  |  |  |  |  |  |  |  |  |
| References |  |  |  |  |  |  |  |  |  |  |
| Research Papers |  |  |  |  |  |  |  |  |  |  |
| Rubrics |  |  |  |  |  |  |  |  |  |  |
| Rules and Procedures Descriptions |  |  |  |  |  |  |  |  |  |  |
| Schedules |  |  |  |  |  |  |  |  |  |  |
| Seating Arrangement Diagrams |  |  |  |  |  |  |  |  |  |  |
| Self-Assessment Instruments |  |  |  |  |  |  |  |  |  |  |

*(continued)*

|  | 1 | 2 | 3 | 4 | 5 | 6 | 7 | 8 | 9 | 10 |
|---|---|---|---|---|---|---|---|---|---|---|
| Simulated Experiences |  |  |  |  |  |  |  |  |  |  |
| Student Contracts |  |  |  |  |  |  |  |  |  |  |
| Student Work |  |  |  |  |  |  |  |  |  |  |
| Teacher-Made Materials |  |  |  |  |  |  |  |  |  |  |
| Technological Resources |  |  |  |  |  |  |  |  |  |  |
| Theme Studies |  |  |  |  |  |  |  |  |  |  |
| Unit Plans |  |  |  |  |  |  |  |  |  |  |
| Video Scenario Critiques |  |  |  |  |  |  |  |  |  |  |
| Volunteer Experience Descriptions |  |  |  |  |  |  |  |  |  |  |
| Work Experience Descriptions |  |  |  |  |  |  |  |  |  |  |

# Developing Your "Portfolio at a Glance"

Developing a brochure will provide interviewers with a "Portfolio at a Glance" that highlights specific teaching behaviors and artifacts that are reflective of your professional development. With such a document, reviewers will be able to focus quickly on what you can do. This section will provide step-by-step directions for developing the brochure. Directions for this type of brochure are for the purpose of providing an example and not meant to imply that there is only one correct way to show a portfolio at a glance.

## Getting Started

The development of the brochure can be divided into two procedures: writing and assembling. Steps 1 through 6 will explain how to write the brochure, and steps 7 through 9 will explain how to assemble the brochure.

### Writing the Brochure

1. REFLECT on one standard at a time.
2. SELECT at least one artifact to feature within a standard.
3. FOCUS on the teaching behaviors that are evidenced in the one artifact.
4. REWORD your teaching behaviors into concise, specific statements in the past tense.
5. CLARIFY your teaching behaviors by writing directly above the name of the artifact a short descriptor of the competency demonstrated.
6. CONTINUE steps 1 through 5 for each standard.

**Assembling the Brochure**

7. CUT and PASTE the list of information using a larger piece of paper or a computer.
8. EDIT the contents of your draft brochure.
9. SELECT desktop design software that will assemble your text to catch the reader's eye.

# Writing the Brochure

1. REFLECT on one standard at a time. Although you will reflect on each of the standards, it will be easiest to begin with the one with which you feel most comfortable. You might, for example, want to start with INTASC Standard Three, which focuses on adapting instruction for individual needs. Write this standard as a concise title.

   Example:   **ADAPTING INSTRUCTION**

2. SELECT at least one artifact within a standard that you wish to have available at interviews. Although you may select several artifacts for a standard, these directions will focus on the selection of one. The artifact that you select should be one of which you are most proud. For example, suppose one artifact you have listed under Standard Three features writing process contracts done on an individual basis. You spent a great deal of time listening and talking with each student in order to address individual needs. You decided this is an ideal artifact to showcase in your brochure. Write a name for the artifact that you select. For example, if you decide to use the title "writing process contracts," you should write that beneath the shortened form of the standard.

   Example:   **ADAPTING INSTRUCTION**
   *Writing Process Contracts*

3. FOCUS on the teaching behaviors that are evidenced in an artifact. As you read over the artifact, ask yourself questions that will help you focus on demonstrated teaching behaviors: What did I do in this lesson? How were my objectives reached? What process did I use to reach my objectives? How were my students engaged? What did I learn to do? By answering such questions, you begin to notice that your writing process contracts reflect several teaching behaviors. More specifically, your objectives were reached because you were able to ADAPT writing segments for ESL (English as a second language) students, PACE content for individual success, ENHANCE clarity through the use of individual resources, and IMPLEMENT teacher modeling and peer sharing to encourage student progress. Write down these important behavioral indicators of your teaching competence.

4. REWORD your teaching behaviors into concise, specific statements in the past tense. Sometimes this may be easy because your original word choices in the rationale and artifact were especially descriptive. At other times this may be the most difficult task in developing the brochure. Brainstorming with others or keeping a simple word list of descriptors by your side may help you select the precise word that is needed. A short word list like the following may help you get started: *adapted, administered, appraised, compiled, constructed, converted, coordinated, created, designed, developed, encouraged, engaged, enhanced, evaluated, expanded, explained, formulated, generated, implemented, integrated, interpreted, mobilized, organized, paced, planned, prioritized, produced, provided, redesigned, related, reorganized, researched, selected, sequenced, translated, utilized,* and *wrote.* Whatever verb you select, it should describe YOUR demonstrated teaching behaviors. Each artifact will probably reflect more than one behavior.

Let's go back to our example. When developing the writing process contracts, your teaching involved four key behaviors. You ADAPTED writing assignments for ESL students, PACED content for individual success, ENHANCED clarity through the use of individual resources, and IMPLEMENTED teacher modeling and peer sharing to encourage student progress. Write down these statements. You now have a list of teacher behaviors that can be listed beneath the two headings, "Adapting Instruction" and "Writing Process Contracts" in your brochure.

Example:   **ADAPTING INSTRUCTION**
 *Writing Process Contracts*
 • Adapted writing assignment for ESL/LEP students
 • Paced content for individual success
 • Utilized individual resources to enhance clarity
 • Implemented teacher modeling and peer sharing to encourage student progress

5. CLARIFY your teaching behaviors by writing, above the name of the artifact, a short descriptor of the competency being demonstrated. Although this step may appear out of sequence, you will be able to accomplish this more easily now than you would have earlier. Look back over the list of teaching behaviors. Ask yourself one question: What did these behaviors enable me to do? In the case of the writing process contracts, you adapted, paced, enhanced, and implemented in order to show that you were "Meeting Individual Needs." Write down this statement in "-ing" form above the name of the artifact to summarize your teaching behaviors.

Example:   **ADAPTING INSTRUCTION**
 **MEETING INDIVIDUAL NEEDS**
 *Writing Process Contracts*

- Adapted writing assignments for ESL/LEP students
- Paced content for individual success
- Utilized individual resources to enhance clarity
- Implemented teacher modeling and peer sharing to encourage student progress

6. CONTINUE steps 1 through 5 for each standard. When you finish, you will have an effective summary of your work in each standard: first, a shortened form of the standard; second, a teaching competency descriptor; third, the name of the artifact; and fourth, a list of teaching behaviors.

## Assembling the Brochure

7. CUT and PASTE the list of information on a larger piece of paper. This will serve as a draft of your final brochure. Paper as large as 11" × 17" will provide greatest flexibility as you position your information. When summarizing work in the ten INTASC standards, it works well to fold the paper twice vertically into a total of three equal sections (six equal sections counting front and back). Close so that it opens like a book with the left section on top. This top section will be the title page of your brochure and should contain introductory information. For example, at the top of this section you could type "Portfolio at a Glance"; in the middle of this section you could attach a photograph of you and your students working together; and at the bottom you could type your name, address, phone number, and email address. The visual impact of this cover should beckon the reader to open your brochure. The remaining five sections of your brochure will accommodate the ten standards—two standards on each section (see the sample brochure). As you open your brochure flat, information for each of the standards should be cut and pasted in sequential order.

8. EDIT the contents of your draft. Double-check the contents to make sure that you've guided readers to what's important. Your brochure should reflect a positive, professional image of your teaching abilities in a concise form.

9. SELECT computer software that will assemble your text to catch the reader's eye. Programs such as Microsoft Publisher, PageMaker, Microsoft Word, and Adobe Type Manager have assisted students in producing a front-to-back, three-column brochure. Whatever software you select, check to make sure that the graphic design helps to communicate effectively what you've worked so hard to produce.

# PORTFOLIO AT A GLANCE

## Jane A. Student

555 Any Street
Anytown, STATE 55555
(555)555-5555
Student@anynet.com

## Instructional Planning Skills

### Using Knowledge of Students

*Teaching Log*
- Administered an interest survey to determine interests and attitudes of a reading buddy in a third-grade classroom
- Administered a running record to determine reading abilities of a third grader
- Planned twelve lessons for a reading buddy based on the literacy needs and interests of the child

### Using Knowledge of Curriculum Goals

*"Theory into Practice Project"*
- Held planning session with teacher to discuss objectives and goals of Medieval Times unit
- Planned a two-part lesson that taught four specific language arts objectives from the district curriculum guide

## Assessment of Student Learning

### Utilizing Informal Assessment

*Moon Journal*
- Provided an ongoing assessment record that monitored student progress
- Evaluated actual student performance

### Planning a Self-Assessment Strategy

*Creative Writing Project*
- Enabled students to reflect and refine their work
- Taught the writing process
- Taught students how to set goals for writing

## Professional Commitment and Responsibility

### Practicing Self-Reflection

*Teaching Log*
- Wrote self-reflective statements for twelve lessons
- Explained professional growth in twelve lessons
- Made plans for future lesson improvement

### Participation in Professional Organizations

*Reading Council Committee Work*
- Helped start a new NCTE affiliate
- Served on the program planning committee

## Partnerships

### Working with Parents/Caregivers

*Afterschool Tutoring Program*
- Tutored students at the PTO-sponsored program
- Located resources and created materials for parent volunteers
- Trained parents and older adults in teaching strategies

### Visiting Other Learning Environments

*Community Site Visits*
- Visited parent partnership programs, hospital crisis centers for children, and rehabilitation centers
- Interviewed parents/caregivers regarding the education and well-being of students

## Knowledge of Subject Matter

### Teaching History

*Unit of Study on Oregon Trail*
- Incorporated primary source material into unit of study
- Taught concepts in a manner consistent with how the research says history should be taught to students
- Included numerous related children's works of fiction and nonfiction

### Collecting and Reporting Data

*Oral History Project*
- Researched history of industry in Green Valley
- Wrote interview protocol
- Conducted oral interview with selected residents of a coal patch town
- Analyzed and reported results of oral histories

## Knowledge of Human Development and Learning

### Valuing Developmental Factors

*Personal Philosophy of Education*
- Described importance of understanding human development
- Illustrated the importance of matching curriculum content and strategies to developmental needs

### Assessing Developmental Readiness

*Case Study*
- Described one student's social, physical, cognitive, and language attainments
- Prescribed developmentally appropriate tasks to enhance this student's development
- Implemented several developmentally appropriate tasks
- Described how the domains affected each other

## Adapting Instruction

### Meeting Individual Needs

*Writing Process Contracts*
- Adapted writing assignment for ESL/LEP students
- Paced content for individual success
- Utilized individual resources to enhance clarity
- Implemented teacher modeling and peer sharing to encourage student progress

### Varying Teaching Strategies

*Lesson Plans*
- Wrote adaptation for special needs students
- Evaluated the effectiveness of the adaptation

## Multiple Instructional Strategies

### Integrating Subject Matter

*Silkworm Rearing Project*
- Created useful activities for many different subject areas
- Encouraged the use of related children's literature

### Using Technology

*Intel ProShare Collaboration*
- Utilized outside resources for lesson enhancement
- Taught students how to create WebQuests

## Classroom Motivation and Management Skills

### Promoting Active Engagement

*Card File of Poetry*
- Gave incentive to use poetry
- Encouraged individual and group motivation
- Created meaningful activities to go along with different types of poems

### Encouraging a Cooperative Learning Environment

*Resource Unit on Seasons*
- Utilized interest groups as well as heterogeneous base groups
- Encouraged the sharing of resources and information

## Communication Skills

### Utilizing Modeling Techniques

*Creative Story*
- Redesigned a popular folktale to model the writing process
- Used intuitive thinking as an affective interactive device

### Presenting Content through Multimedia

*Multimedia Compilation*
- Produced pertinent examples of educational media
- Used popular topics to promote greater student interaction

APPENDIX

D

# Glossary

**Artifact**   Tangible evidence that indicates an achievement of a goal or the attainment of knowledge and skills, such as professional work samples, videos, letters, student products, or certificates.

**Authentic assessment**   A performance assessment that measures your ability to apply understanding in authentic contexts; assignments that involve real-world problem solving or serve a meaningful purpose in a real-life situation.

**Interstate New Teacher Assessment and Support Consortium (INTASC)**   A consortium of more than thirty states operating under the Council of Chief State School Officials that has developed standards and is designing an assessment process for initial teacher certification.

**INTASC Standards**   A set of expectations applicable for beginning teachers of all disciplines and grade levels developed by the Interstate New Teacher Assessment and Support Consortium.

**National Board for Professional Teaching Standards (NBPTS)**   A board created to achieve two primary purposes: developing standards in many fields for what accomplished teachers should know and be able to do and developing a voluntary national credential for accomplished teachers that includes the presentation of portfolios based on these standards.

**Portfolio at a Glance**   A brochure you create to summarize the documents in your presentation portfolio.

**Presentation portfolio**   A carefully selected, streamlined, and organized collection of work samples and other pieces of evidence prepared to share with others, especially with those making judgments about your achieved competence.

**Rationale**   An explanation of your reasoning for the inclusion of a portfolio artifact. It summarizes the document and experiences, explains their value for professional development, and describes implications for future work.

**Standards**   Expected learning outcomes that delineate the key aspects of professional performance.

**Working portfolio**   A portfolio that is organized around standards and contains the complete collection of past work in unabridged form as well as work in progress.